START
A **CAREER**
WITH
PYTHON

A hands-on step-by-step guide for the
complete beginner with real life examples

by **Pedro Rodrigues**

Start a Career with Python
by Pedro Rodrigues

Visit the book's website at https://www.startacareerwithpython.com.

First edition

To Shirley.

Acknowledgements

The completion of this book has a special meaning to me, because not only it allowed me to tick off an item from a very old *To Do* list, but also because I wrote the book I wish I had read when I started my first steps in programming many years ago. Or, at least, I tried to write such a book.

Not everyone who is dear to me had an important role, so without beating around the bush I will just acknowledge those who had an impact on the outcome.

Technical Thanks

I enjoy a lot programming in many different languages, but no other language gave me the urge to write a book as much as Python did. Python, as a language and as a community, played a very important role and made it possible not only for me to have fun while writing a book but also to (hopefully) help and be useful to whoever reads it.

I'm definitely grateful to my girlfriend Shirley for everything she is and for her invaluable contribution to this book, with her eagle eye for attention, her perfectionism and her perspective of someone with no experience in IT.

It's also worth mentioning the effort that my friend Joana Peixoto put in the initial stage of the book, providing the perspective of someone who just started taking her first steps into software development. My good friend Marco Lovetere (@marcolovetere) also played an important rule, by providing good insights with his technical expertise and eye for detail.

Any glitches that you may find in this book are my entire responsibility.

Personal Thanks

Besides the technical thanks, there are a couple of other people who are definitely worth mentioning. My parents and my sister, who have always supported me in all my endeavors. And, finally, my friend Joshua Martens (@jcjvm) for constantly giving me fresh ideas.

I can't express how excited I am with the completion of this book. Hopefully you will find programming in Python as fun as I do. I've worked with several programming languages (and still do) and Python is definitely the one I rejoice the most with when developing software. The language was developed in the late 80s by Guido van Rossum and it allows you to express your ideas with clarity and simplicity. Even though you can express the same ideas in fewer lines of code when compared to languages like Java or C++, the language is widely used to solve real world and complex problems, and its popularity has been increasing.

One of the main reasons that made me choose Python as a language for the complete beginner who wants to delve into software development is that learning should be fun. Don't get me wrong, I find it fun as well writing software in Java or C. But with Python you can dive much faster into solving interesting problems rather than having to worry about the quirks of the language itself. It may not be the best choice if you want to develop software made for high performance, but if you are a complete beginner, this will definitely not be the first task you will be assigned. In any case, as soon as you used Python enough to explore and understand concepts of Computer Science, you will feel much more comfortable to start tackling much more complex problems, which will eventually lead you to learn other languages and technologies. In fact, you should definitely expand your skillset with languages that vary in their design and paradigms. Languages of a lower level like C (or even lower, like Assembly) will make you appreciate all the high level constructs provided by Python, since those languages provide none out of the box. Languages like Lisp or Haskell will force you to think in a different way when writing software, due to their underlying paradigm. At the end of the day, you should feel comfortable writing software with at least 2 or 3 programming languages, but you'll definitely find your favorite along the journey. I've found mine!

Who Is This Book For

I wrote this book with the motivation of helping other people making a career switch to Software Development using Python. As such, I expect the majority of the readers to be people who have got no experience or background in IT or Software Development.

Programmers who come from other languages and want to make a transition to Python may find the materials in this book useful. Nonetheless, I hope they will bear with me and don't despair when I spend a fair amount of time explaining certain concepts, which will strike them as obvious and immediate. I recognize that, for the experienced programmer, skipping certain sections will not only be tempting but completely understandable.

What You Will Learn

If you want to start a career as a software developer (or if you want to start developing software in your spare time), you will have to learn more than just the syntax of a programming language. In this book, I will give you an overview of the most common tools and required skills in a typical ecosystem of software development.

This is supposed to be a step-by-step guide, so each chapter (in the form of a step) will be used as a building block for understanding the concepts explained in further chapters. I also expect you to start developing the kind of mindset that is common amongst computer programmers and hackers, and do your own (and thorough) research, either whenever something is not fully understood or when you want to expand your knowledge on a certain topic.

> **Note**: I'm using the term hacker according to the definition found in Eric Raymond's How-To, not according to the misleading definition spread out by certain media:
>
> *The members of this culture originated the term 'hacker'. Hackers built the Internet. Hackers made the Unix operating system what it is today. Hackers make the World Wide Web work. If you are part of this culture, if you have contributed to it and other people in it know who you are and call you a hacker, you're a hacker.*
>
> You can (and should) read the entire How-To *How to Become a Hacker*[1].

Certain subjects have their own importance, but were deliberately left unwritten since they are outside the scope of this book. By the moment you finish reading the book, you will have enough knowledge for writing relatively complex Python programs and for continuing your journey on your own.

STEP 1 – UNDERSTANDING THE BASICS

This step is intended to help you hit the ground running. To fully take advantage of what you are about to learn regarding Python, you must first learn the concepts explained in this step. I will cover some of the most important topics you would learn in a Computer Science course, just with enough detail to get you going. You will first be introduced to what an Operating System and the Kernel are. I will also tell you about the basics of the command-line, as it will be your working environment in the next pages. Binary and Hexadecimal numeral systems will be explained with plenty of examples, as well as the importance and the roles of the CPU and Memory. The main Data Structures will be exposed and I finish this step with basic concepts of Computer Networking. By the end of *Step 1*, you'll feel more confident and you'll be able to grasp the concepts in the future steps without much trouble.

STEP 2 – JUMPING HEAD FIRST INTO PYTHON

As soon as you have the necessary knowledge to progress and no longer feel like a complete beginner, it's time to dive into Python. **Practice makes perfect**, so this step will involve having you playing around with the command-line, the Python interpreter and the interactive shell. You will learn the main Python data types, operators, control flow constructs, how to define your own functions, how to handle exceptions and errors and concepts of Object Oriented and Functional Programming. You will be challenged to solve some problems that will range from extremely simple to somewhat difficult. I will also teach you how to think like a computer scientist, by explaining the reasoning behind certain solutions to problems I propose. You are expected to make experiments as you read.

STEP 3 – USING VERSION CONTROL SYSTEMS: GIT

At this point you are already acquainted with most of the main concepts of Python. You can already read fairly complex code and make some sense out of it. But, if in the future you are going to collaborate with other people (or even if you want to have your work publicly available), you need to know what others (or at least most of them) are using for collaboration and version control. In this step you will learn some key principles behind Git and how to use it with your own projects.

You may be wondering how can Python be applied in real world? This step guides you through some of the many applications of Python and hopefully will spark some curiosity and make you explore even further. Research the things I mention in this step, get your hands dirty, try to think of a project and incorporate some of the concepts learned here.

You've finished the book. Now what? Now it's time for you to walk the path (mostly) alone. Either by contributing to Open Source projects or by participating in programming competitions or working on your own projects. There are many ways for you to become proficient and always up-to-date. In this step I will point you in the right direction.

Limitations of This Book

This book won't help you master Python in one day, like some books claim. That's impossible. **Practice makes perfect**, so I assume you will get your hands dirty and make experiments on your own. This is also not a complete guide to the Python language. I won't cover exhaustively all the libraries and features of the language. You can and should check the official Python documentation for that and use it as a reference. I deliberately didn't cover all the aspects of any of the topics in this book, even though this book is supposed to be self-contained and have everything you need to build your first application. All the technical jargon and buzzwords you come across will be at least briefly explained in the book.

This book does not attempt to show all the possible solutions to a problem. When developing software, you can always take several approaches. Some are simpler, less optimal and yet allow you to have a faster time-to-market. Others are much more robust, scalable, but far more complex and take too much time to implement. Others are somewhere in between. When you develop software for a company, especially a startup, you will always have to make hard decisions. You'll either be short on people, short on money or short on time. Hopefully you won't be short on more than 2 of these at the same time. These constraints will determine which direction you should take when developing software.

Conventions used

Hopefully, the purpose of using different fonts in this book will strike you as obvious, as well as its meaning in the specific context. Nonetheless, a few notes worth mentioning:

- `This font` is used to express either values, variables, constants or module names.
- Certain verbs in bold indicate a function or method, like **print** or **open**.
- Inside boxes, **>>>** indicates the prompt in Python interpreter, where you are supposed to put code and hit the *Enter* key. When you hit *Enter*, whatever appears in the following line is the result of interpreting the command entered by you, unless the line starts with a multi-line prefix.
- Inside boxes, **. . .** indicates multi-line Python code.
- The symbol ↵ indicates line wrapping.
- Inside certain boxes, ➜ `~/StartCareerPython` indicates the prompt in the terminal / shell. My prompt is customized, a bit different from the default one. Typical prompts in Terminal are:
  `Pedros-macbook:~ StartCareerPython$`

9

This indicates that I am currently in the directory **StartCareerPython**.

Using Code Examples

You are free to use the code provided in this book as you wish, with no constraints. The code is available as a Zip or Tar file:

- https://www.startacareerwithpython.com/book_code.zip
- https://www.startacareerwithpython.com/book_code.tar.gz

How to Get in Touch

. **Email:** pedro@startacareerwithpython.com.
. **Website:** http://www.startacareerwithpython.com.
Make sure to subscribe to the newsletter, as I will be sharing tips and tricks, articles and tutorials that you can use complementary to the book.
. **Twitter:** @pe__d__ro

Introduction

Developing software is far from being an easy task, unless you write small and basic code. In general, not only you need to keep in mind the rules inherent in the language you use but also the rules inherent in the software you are writing. Unless you aren't worried about your future self, you need to make certain decisions at a very early stage by foreseeing all the potential scenarios and corner cases that you or the end user will run into. The architectural decisions you make today will determine the amount of time and effort that you (or whoever is assigned the task) will have in the future to extend functionalities, make changes or fix bugs in the software you wrote.

The clarity, consistency and coherence of your code can be what determines if you will spend one hour fixing a bug instead of one day or more. The structure of your code determines if adding a new functionality is as easy as just adding a couple more lines of code or if you need to rewrite a big part of the application.

WHAT CAN YOU DO AS A SOFTWARE DEVELOPER?

Many things you use on a daily basis have some sort of software that was written by one or more people. The apps that you use on your smartphone to check your emails, instant messages or listen to music were developed by mobile engineers. If they are apps for Android, they required at least knowledge of Java and Android SDK, whereas if they are apps for iPhone they require at least knowledge of Objective-C. The software that allows you to schedule your washing machine to complete a 40-minute program at 50º C in 3 hours was probably developed by embedded software developers. The same goes for the software that controls robot vacuum cleaners or cars. The software that you use to create the working schedule of your employees in your restaurant was probably built by one or more web developers with experience in HTML, CSS and JavaScript (and probably PHP and some sort of database).

Apps like Twitter, Facebook, Instagram, Airbnb or Uber have huge multi-disciplinary teams behind them, such as network and security engineers, data scientists, full stack software developers, mobile software engineers, cloud applications engineers, etc. Even if you are not a full time software developer, you can still use programming languages on a daily basis to assist you in your work. For example, chemists or biologists often use programming languages (Python, many times) in order to automate experiments or process measurement results.

GETTING READY FOR THE ADVENTURE

With this in mind, it's time for you to get ready and psychologically prepared for the adventure you have ahead!

Many professions require you to be constantly learning, and as a software developer you will be studying and learning more often than not. It's an extremely fast paced industry, where technological advantage sometimes means everything. It's not just about having the best idea or the best financial support, but also about having the best tech and the best techies. And the best techies are those that help build the most secure or fastest or most scalable, robust or dependable (or all of those and even more) software. They do that because they are able to think out of the box, because they gained experience and know when to use the right tool for the job. And if there is no right tool yet, they will invent it. It takes time and practice, but it's not impossible for you to get to this point, even if you are a complete beginner, as I expect you to be. And when you get to that point, your computer will no longer be seen as a black box where magic happens inside, but as a tool that you can use and control (almost) at your will.

As you progress in this book, I expect that you'll grasp or fully understand the code snippets before reading my explanations. But if this doesn't happen, don't despair, because some people may take more time than others, which is perfectly fine and normal. When I studied Computer Science, it took me a bit to understand Prolog (another programming language). As soon as it makes a click in your brain, you will be able to read code as you would read a book. Unless the code is a mess, of course, but that also happens with certain books.

Step 1 – Warming up with the basics

Before you get your hands on Python, there are a few things you must learn. These are concepts you will be dealing with either on a daily basis or regularly enough for you to not skip them. Having this knowledge will be fundamental and can save you many headaches and also many hours of your precious time doing research.

So, without any further delay, this is what you'll have learned by the end of this chapter:

- What an **Operating System** and its **Kernel** are
- Basics of the **command-line**
- **Binary** and **Hexadecimal** numeral systems
- Some **bitwise operations**: **NOT, AND, OR, XOR** and **shift**
- What the **CPU** and **main memory (RAM)** are.
- What a **data structure** is and how to use it (Lists, Dictionaries, Hash Tables, Queues, Stacks, etc)
- What an **algorithm** is
- What an **IP Address** is and some differences between **IPv4** and **IPv6**
- What a **DNS** server is and its main role

1.1 The Operating System

An Operating System is the software that allows you to make use of the hardware of your computer. It manages the hardware and software resources and provides common services for the computer programs. Without an Operating

System, you wouldn't be able to use the software you use on a daily basis. Assuming you fall in the category of my main target, I expect you to be using some version of Windows or Mac OS X... or maybe even Linux.

1.1.1 The Kernel

The applications you install are just a bunch of files lying on the hard drive of your computer. Besides taking up storage space, they don't do much more. It's only when you run them that they become "alive". In order for an application to become "alive", a *process* must be created. A *process* is the execution environment for a running program and it contains the code of the program itself, the data it uses, etc. There is a special software called *kernel*, which is the core of the Operating System, that creates and manages the *processes*, memory and is aware of everything that happens in the system.

1.1.2 Using the command-line

The term command-line refers to a way of interacting with your computer (or a computer program) by issuing commands in the form of successive lines of text, which are the command lines. In Windows, you can do this via the PowerShell and in Mac OS X you can do this via the Terminal. In Linux, depending on the Desktop Manager you use (Gnome, Unity, KDE, etc) it may have different names. Of course, if you are not using any Desktop or Window Manager, then you are most likely in the command-line already.

Throughout the book, you'll be using the command-line extensively, so I'll make sure to cover some aspects that will be important. I am working in Mac OS X, so my examples will use Terminal app for accessing the command line. You can launch it via *Spotlight* or by going to *Finder > Applications > Utilities > Terminal*.

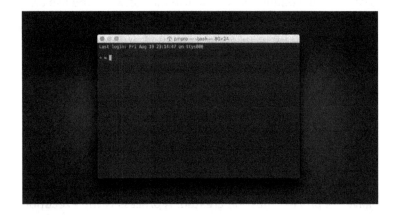

When you open a Terminal, you will be presented with information regarding your last login date and a prompt, waiting for you to enter commands. The prompt may vary (you can tweak its aspect), though. The Terminal app is actually starting another program which is a *command-line interpreter*, often referred to as a *shell*.

The *shell* hides the details of the underlying Operating System and provides constructs and commands that allow you to create and manipulate files, execute programs, manipulate programs input and output, amongst many other things. It basically provides you a simpler interface that allows you to interact with the Operating System and its Kernel.

There are many shells to choose from. In my case, I am using *Bash*, or **Bourne** *again* **shell**, which is the default shell in Mac OS X. *Bash* is a shell but also a *scripting language*, that provides similar features to what Python provides. Shells rely on *environment variables* (which are names that store specific data) for many operations. These environment variables are like some sort of Yellow Pages that the *shell* uses. Let's see an example:

I entered `aaaaa` and the shell replied, saying that the command was not found. When you type something and press the *Enter* key, the shell will first check if it's a built-in command from the shell itself. In case it is, the command is interpreted and an output is generated. In case it isn't, the shell interpreter will look for a file with the name of the command in some locations. These locations are stored in an environment variable, called `PATH`. `PATH` holds a list of directories that contain executable files of programs. This environment variable comes with a default list of locations, but you can modify and add custom locations yourself. If the command is not found in these locations, then a `command not found` error is generated as an output.

There are plenty of environment variables that serve different purposes and you can also create them and use in your programs. Throughout the book, I will introduce you to more shell commands and a couple of environment variables. If you understood what was explained so far, you'll do just fine!

1.2 Numeral systems

Numeral systems are a written form for expressing numbers of a given set, which can be the set of all *integers* or the set of all *rational numbers*, for example. If you're wondering what an *integer* is, it's a number that can be written without a fractional component (e.g. -5, 21, -43, 0). A numeral system uses digits (from 0 to 9) and / or other symbols to express those numbers. For the sake of simplicity, we'll only deal with positive integers including zero (0).

Most people only deal with the *decimal* numeral system, which they learn in school and continue to use it throughout their lives. The *decimal* numeral system uses digits from 0 to 9 to express the numbers. The digit 0 represents the integer 0, and the group of digits 143 represents the integer 143. You never think about it, that's just the way it is. With one single position you can represent up to 10 different integers, ranging from 0 to 9. With two positions, you can represent up to 100 different integers, ranging from 0 to 99. A way of thinking about it is that you can have 10 times 10 different digits:

P2	P1
0	0
0	1
0	...
0	9
1	0
...	...
9	9

P1 refers to the digit in the first position (right) and P2 refers to the digit in the second position (left). The reason why I'm explaining something that is so obvious is because the two numeral systems I'm going to introduce next actually require you to understand this underlying logic. If you take a look at the table above, you'll see that the digits in the second position progress slower than the first one: they change every ten first digits. If you use 3 positions, you can represent up to 1000 different integers. If we had a similar table, you would see that the digits in the third position progress even slower: every 10 changes of the second position or every 100 changes of the first position.

So with 3 positions you can represent up to $10\times10\times10$ different integers, which is 10^3. With N positions you can represent up to 10^N different integers, which range from 0 to $10^N - 1$. Right? So far, you haven't learned anything new, and hopefully you are just seeing what you already knew from a different perspective. *Decimal* numeral system is also called *base 10*, because it uses 10 different symbols (the digits from 0 to 9).

1.2.1 Binary numeral system

Binary numeral system is almost always immediately associated with computers, even though such a system has been around since ancient civilizations.

It is used by almost all modern computers because of the way they work. 0 and 1 are an abstraction used to represent the two different voltage bands associated with the signals that digital circuits handle. Unlike the decimal numeral system, binary numbering only uses two digits: 0 and 1. Because of that, it's also known as *base 2*. Even though this may seem a bit confusing at first, the principle is the same as the decimal numeral system: you are expressing numbers of a given set. When you use the decimal numeral system to represent numbers from the set of integers, you don't need to make any conversion to see which value you are representing: the decimal number 12 represents the integer 12, just like 923 represents 923. This doesn't apply to binary numeral system, where 11 represents the integer 3, even though it uses the same digits as the decimal number 11. Let's understand why!

How many different integers can you represent using 1 position in decimal numeral system? 10, right? Because you have 10 different digits, you can represent integers from 0 to 9. In binary, with one position you can represent 2 different integers: 0 and 1. So, 0 in binary has the same value as 0 in decimal and 1 in binary has the same value as 1 in decimal. So far so good. So if you want to represent more integers, you need to use more positions:

P3	P2	P1	Decimal value
0	0	0	0
0	0	1	1
0	1	0	2
0	1	1	3
1	0	0	4
1	0	1	5
1	1	0	6
1	1	1	7

If the binary number has 2 positions, you can represent up to 4 integers. With 3 positions, you can represent 8 integers from 0 to 7. You also easily understand how the binary numbers progress, by using the same logic as with decimal numbers: when you exhaust all the bits from the first position (a digit in binary numeral system is referred to as a *bit*), you increment the second position and restart the sequence on the first one. With N bits you can represent up to 2^N different integers, that range from 0 to $2^N - 1$ (**note**: remember that, for the sake of simplicity, we are only considering positive integers, including zero).

If you didn't understand how I got to this, just use the same method as with decimal numeral system! With 1 bit you represent up to 2 integers. With 2 bits, you represent up to 2×2 (or 2^2) integers. With 3 bits you represent up to $2\times2\times2$ (or 2^3) integers. It's not that hard, right?

By the way, in computer science a group of 8 *bits* is called a *byte*.

Bitwise Operations

Since it's quite frequent to think in terms of bits and bit patterns in computing, it's also very common to perform operations on those same bits. They are called *bitwise operations*.

Bitwise operations are much faster when compared to arithmetic operations such as division, multiplication, addition and subtraction. I will be introducing you to a few of them and, as you progress and feel the need, you will be able to explore and learn others.

For the following operations, the digits 0 and 1 won't behave like the integers *0* and *1*. Instead they will be treated like the truth values False and True, respectively. Also, the positions of the bits, whenever mentioned in the text, will be counted from right (*least significant bit*) to left (*most significant bit*). This order of counting (and also of storing information) is called **little-endian**. So, for example, in the binary number 0001, the digit 1 occurs in the first position and is said to be the *least significant bit*.

I've found that associating the bits 0 and 1 to the state of a lamp makes it easier for people to grasp bitwise operations. Let's then see if it's also easier for you, and imagine that 0 represents the state when the light is *off* and 1 means that the light is *on*. Let's also pretend that you have an app in your phone that shows the state of the lamps of your **bedroom (BR)**, **kitchen (KC)**, **living room (LR)** and **bathroom (BA)**.

	BR	KC	LR	BA
State	0	0	0	0

We'll start with all lights switched off!

NOT

The bitwise **NOT** performs *logical* negation on each bit, meaning that a 1 becomes a 0 and a 0 becomes a 1.

A	NOT A
0	1
1	0

For example, the integer *13* can be represented by the binary number 1101. Which means that after the operation **NOT**, it will become the integer 2:

NOT 1101 = 0010 (integer *2*)

Let's think of our little app that shows the state of the lights. At some point, the lights of the bedroom, kitchen and bathroom are on. The lights of the living room are off:

	BR	KC	LR	BA
State	1	1	0	1

The binary number `1101` (or the decimal 13) represents the current state of the lights. After the **NOT** bitwise operation, the lights of the living room will be on and all the others will be off.

	BR	KC	LR	BA
State	0	0	1	0

AND

The bitwise **AND** takes two operands with the same length and performs logical **AND** operation to every pair of bits according to the following table:

A	B	A AND B
0	0	0
0	1	0
1	0	0
1	1	1

This can be translated to "the truth value of the expression **A AND B** is `True` if both propositions A and B are `True`, otherwise it is `False`". Let's see the bitwise AND between 27 and 13 in action:

(27)	1	1	0	1	1
(13)	0	1	1	0	1
(9)	0	1	0	0	1

Because the two operands must have the same length, I added a leading 0 (zero) to 13. This is called *left padding*. The resulting number can't be related to any of the arithmetic operations you are used to. This is merely the result of a logical operation. Bitwise AND operations are extremely useful for *masking* bits. In order for me to explain what *masking* is, let's go back to the lights example. We still have the lights in the bedroom, kitchen and bathroom switched on. For some reason, you want to make sure that the lights in the bedroom and the bathroom are always off. How can you enforce that? You can perform a bitwise **AND** between your current state and a *mask*. In this case the *mask* is 0110. Let's see an example:

	BR	KC	LR	BA
Old State	1	1	0	1
Mask	0	1	1	0
New State	0	1	0	0

If you recall the bitwise **AND** table, whenever you **AND** any bit with 0, the result is 0. So, if you want to enforce certain bits to be 0 and not affect the others, just create a *mask* with 0s in the positions you want to affect and 1s in the remaining positions.

Bitwise AND is also an extremely fast way to check the *parity* of a number (to check whether a number is even or not). How do we do that? Well, if you write any integer in binary numeral system, you will notice that every odd integer has the digit *1* in the first position, whereas every even number has the digit *0* instead. Don't believe me? Give it a try! The integer 10 is 1010 in binary. The integer 27 is 11011. What about 1042 and 211? Surprise! They are 10000010010 and 11010011, respectively. Which means that we can use bitwise **AND** between any number and binary 1: if the result is 0, then the number is even, if the result is 1 then the number is odd.

(27)	1	1	0	1	1
Mask	0	0	0	0	1
Result	0	0	0	0	1

Since the result is 1, then 27 is odd. Of course you don't need to have this trouble when you know the number, but when you are writing software you will be dealing with many dynamic values that you don't know beforehand, so you will have to do certain things programmatically.

OR

The bitwise **OR** also takes two operands of equal length, but behaves in a slightly different way: the expression is 1 if at least one of the operands is 1, otherwise it's 0.

A	B	A OR B
0	0	0
0	1	1
1	0	1
1	1	1

Here's an example of OR operation between the integers 14 and 27:

(27)	1	1	0	1	1
(14)	0	1	1	1	0
(31)	1	1	1	1	1

The bitwise **OR** is useful when you want to set certain bits to 1. Now, let's say that instead of keeping the lights in the bedroom and bathroom always off, you actually want to keep them always on. Instead of using a bitwise **AND**, you use a bitwise **OR**. And the mask now is 1001 instead of 0110. Recall the **OR** logical table: bitwise **OR** between any bit and 1 is always 1. Bitwise **OR** between any bit and 0 is always the other bit. We'll start with the state 0101 (lights in the bedroom and living room are off, all the rest is on):

	BR	KC	LR	BA
Old State	0	1	0	1
Mask	1	0	0	1
New State	1	1	0	1

XOR

The bitwise operator **XOR**, or *exclusive OR*, also takes two operands with the same length and works the following way: the result of the operation is 1 if the corresponding bits are different, otherwise it's 0.

A	B	A XOR B
0	0	0
0	1	1
1	0	1
1	1	0

I believe you're already starting to get a grip on this, so why don't you calculate **21 XOR 7** and **3 XOR 14**?

This operation has interesting properties and can be used, for example, to toggle certain bits (or invert, or flip, however you want to call). In order to toggle a bit, you need to **XOR** it with 1. This time, we want to toggle the light in the kitchen (switch it on if it's off and switch it off if it's on). In order to achieve that, we just need to bitwise **XOR** the current state with 0100.

	BR	KC	LR	BA
Old State	1	1	0	1
Mask	0	1	0	0
New State	1	0	0	1

The light was on and now it's off. If we want to switch it on again, we just **XOR** the new state with the same mask:

	BR	KC	LR	BA
Old State	1	0	0	1
Mask	0	1	0	0
New State	1	1	0	1

Shift

In bitwise **shift** operations, the digits are *shifted* (or moved) to the left or to the right a certain amount of positions. When you perform a **shift left**, a zero is shifted in on the right.

Let's see what happens when we shift the integer 75 (1001011 in binary) both left and right, 1 and 2 positions on each case:

	Shift left-one	Shift left-two	Shift right-one	Shift right-two
1001011	1001011**0**	1001011**00**	0100101	0010010

The interesting thing to notice is that when you shift left one position, the resulting bit pattern represents an integer whose value is twice the original: `10010110` represents the integer `150`. The binary number `100101100` represents the integer `300`. When you shift a number N positions to the left, you are multiplying that number by 2^N. And a bitwise shift is actually faster than performing a regular arithmetic multiplication, computationally speaking.

1.2.2 Hexadecimal numeral system

Now that you understand the binary numeral system, it won't be hard for you to figure out how hexadecimal numbers represent integers. Hexadecimal numeral system uses 16 different symbols (*base 16*, as you can already guess), namely all the decimal digits from 0 to 9 and the letters **a**, **b**, **c**, **d**, **e** and **f**. These letters represent the integers 10, 11, 12, 13, 14 and 15, respectively. Let's build our table with the decimal equivalence:

P2	P1	Decimal value
0	0	0
0	1	1
..	..	..
0	a	10
0	b	11

..	..	..
0	f	15
1	0	16
1	1	17
..	..	..
1	f	31
...	...	...
f	0	240
...	...	...
f	f	255

The sequence, once again, progresses using the same logic as with the previous numeral systems. But, as you can already notice, with 2 positions you can represent up to 256 different integers, ranging from 0 to 255 (like I've mentioned before, we aren't considering negative numbers for the sake of simplicity).

Again, with N positions, you can represent up to 16^N different integers. In computer science, you'll often see hexadecimal numbers represented with a prefix (or a suffix). Most of the times, they start with **0x** followed by the number itself: **0x**2f or **0x**dead1eaf. The suffix is just a way to tell you that you are dealing with a hexadecimal number, it's not part of the number itself.

So, you've learned that binary and hexadecimal numeral systems represent numbers from a given set, just the same way decimal numeral system does. Most people are used to think in terms of decimal numbers, and because their representation is quite straightforward, we don't exactly need to figure out which integer we are representing. 923 is 923, 11 is 11 and 0 is 0. But with binary and hexadecimal numbers, this is not that immediate, depending on the size of the number and your ability to make arithmetic operations mentally. For example, you know that the binary number 0 represents the integer 0 and the binary number 100 represents the integer 4. If I ask you the same about the binary number 10100, you can still give me an answer, if you have the patience to draw a table with 5 bits and reach the integer 20. But it's not convenient at all. If you want to know the way of finding out which integer a binary or a hexadecimal number represent, then continue reading. The alternative is to just use a calculator that supports "Programmer" view and allows you to switch numeral systems: you first chose the base you want (base 2 or base 16), you write down the number, then you choose base 10 and the conversion is made. That's actually what most programmers do, especially when dealing with big numbers.

In my opinion, the easiest way for you to understand how to find the integer represented by any number is to start with the decimal number itself and decompose it. If you think of any decimal number below 10, there isn't much you can do. If you have the decimal number 22, for instance, you can decompose it into 20 + 2. Just like you can decompose the decimal number 147 into 100 + 40 + 7. Or the number 1473 into 1000 + 400 + 70 + 3. You may have noticed that this follows a pattern, and the base of the numeral system (in this case it is *base 10*) makes part of that pattern. Take a look again at how I decomposed the number 1473:

$$1473 = 1000 + 400 + 70 + 3$$

This is equivalent to having this:

$$1473 = 1 \times 1000 + 4 \times 100 + 7 \times 10 + 3 \times 1$$

Which in turn is the same as having:

$$1473 = 1{\times}10^3 + 4{\times}10^2 + 7{\times}10^1 + 3{\times}10^0$$

So the pattern is actually quite simple: you start counting the position of each digit from right to the left and the counting starts at *0* and goes until *N-1*, where *N* is the number of positions. You multiply each digit by the base of the numeral system powered to the position of the digit (in this case, the base is 10). The end result is the sum of all these multiplications. You would never do this on a daily basis, because the numeral system you use is quite straightforward (it directly maps the integers). If you want to buy a car for $15,000, you don't think "Oh, let me guess what integer that price represents". But if the salesman told you "This car costs $11101010011000, and the price is represented in *base 2*.", then you would need to find the integer and conclude that it was actually $15,000. So, how do you calculate this without resorting to a fancy calculator? Well, you decompose the binary number exactly the same way we decomposed the decimal one. The only difference is that you replace the base 10 by 2 in the multiplications. Let's decompose it now:

$$11101010011000$$

Is equivalent to:

$$1{\times}2^{13} + 1{\times}2^{12} + 1{\times}2^{11} + \cdots + 0{\times}2^0$$

And you would conclude that the salesman was selling you the car for $15,000. And now I challenge you to find out which integer the hexadecimal number `4fc18` represents (confirm your end result with the one you get from converting in a calculator).

1.3 CPU and Memory

Everyone developing software should know at least what the CPU and Memory are. Actually there are several types of memory, but in general when we refer to memory we are speaking about the "main memory", or RAM (*Random Access Memory*). RAM is volatile, meaning that the information it stores will disappear when you shut down your computer.

Besides RAM, there is also secondary memory, which is where your programs and data are kept on a long-term basis, meaning that it's not volatile like RAM. Examples of secondary memory are your hard drive disk, SSD, CDs, DVDs, etc.

The **CPU** (Central Processing Unit) is the brain of your computer, it's the component used to execute your programs and main Memory is the component that stores your program while it's being executed.

For you to better understand memory, think of a bunch of lockers at a gym, where you can store your stuff before you go lift. Each locker has a sequence number and all the lockers have the same storage capacity. Memory is like a bunch of these lockers with sequence numbers, which are referred to as *memory addresses*, and they can store *8 bits* of data, or *1 byte*.

For convenience, memory addresses are often expressed using hexadecimal numbers. This is what a typical memory address looks like: 0x7fff9575c050. Because you can only store 8 bits worth of information in one memory address, sometimes you need to use more than one storage location for one piece of information. For instance, if you want to store a *64-bit* integer you would need to use 8 consecutive memory addresses, since each memory address references an *8-bit* storage location.

The main memory is used to store pretty much anything, from the position of the cursor of your mouse to the graphics of the icons on your desktop or results from calculations.

Main memory is also where your program resides while being executed. Not only your program but also temporary data that it may use and create. The CPU is constantly in a *fetch-and-execute* cycle, where it fetches the next instruction to be executed and executes it, from the moment you switch on your computer to the moment you switch it off.

The CPU also contains another type of memory of much faster access, but smaller in size, when compared to Main Memory. It's called *Cache*. The CPU uses its *Cache* to store copies of data from memory locations that are frequently used, even though most CPUs have separate caches for instructions and data. As a matter of fact, most modern CPUs have multiple levels of cache: L1, L2 and L3. They differ not only in size, but also in access time. Because the CPU Cache is much smaller than Main Memory, its contents are more frequently overridden. When the CPU tries to fetch contents that do not exist in Cache, it's called a *Cache Miss*. If the contents exist in Cache, it's called a *Cache Hit*.

1.4 Data structures

Data structures are used to store data in a particular way, so that it can be accessed and manipulated efficiently.

Different data structures organize the data in different ways and are suitable for specific situations. Even without being aware, you use in real life situations certain data structures that resemble the ones used in Computer Science. For example, when you create a list for your groceries, you are using a... *list*. Most likely you also have a *dictionary* at home. Probably plates in your kitchen cabinet are piled as a *stack*.

Since different data structures organize data in different way, they also provide different methods for accessing and manipulating the data. The majority of the programming languages provides the most common data structures either as a built-in feature or in some module or library. If not, they will provide tools for you to implement such data structures.

1.4.1 Arrays

An **array** is a data structure that is designed to store a collection of objects and lies on consecutive memory addresses. Below you can find a very simple schema of an array that stores 6 elements:

0	1	2	3	4	5
0x7fff9570	0x7fff9571	0x7fff9572	0x7fff9573	0x7fff9574	0x7fff9575

Let's say that this array will store integers that range from 0 to 255. I only need 8 bits to support 256 integers, as you've already learned. Since each memory location stores exactly 8 bits of information, then each bucket of the array matches exactly one memory address. **But this is not always the case!**

Like I said before, if you need to store a *64-bit* integer, you would need 8 consecutive memory addresses. Which means that if you wanted to create an array to store 9 *64-bit* integers, it would take 72 memory storage locations instead of just 9.

In the image above, you can find the memory addresses expressed in hexadecimal: 0x7fff9570 to 0x7fff9575. Above the array buckets you have other sequence numbers starting at zero. These numbers are the array *index* and the counting in general starts at 0. Most of the programming languages follow this counting principle, except for a few languages, like Lua, that start counting on 1. When you refer to the first element of the array, you are referring to the element with index 0. The second element has index 1 and, as you can easily guess, the 6th element has index 5.

Let's suppose that we want to create an array to store *8-bit* lottery numbers:

0	1	2	3	4	5
143	**2**	**15**	**200**	**214**	**119**
0x7fff9570	0x7fff9571	0x7fff9572	0x7fff9573	0x7fff9574	0x7fff9575

The fourth element is number 200, which has index *3* and its memory address is 0x7fff9573. Remember that the memory addresses are consecutive and they represent integers, which means that you can use arithmetic operations as you would use with decimal numbers. The second element is number 2, which has index 1 and its memory address is 0x7fff9571. If you had created an array to store 16-bit lottery numbers instead, it would look slightly different, since each array bucket would take 2 memory addresses instead of just 1. You would use the array indexes just as normally and the arithmetic to calculate the memory addresses of each array element would be the same. The only difference is that the memory address of the next element will be located in *M0 + 2* instead of *M0 + 1*, where M0 is the memory address of the current element. This is because each array element takes up 2 memory locations instead of just 1. When you use arrays you refer to its elements using the index, so you won't need to worry about their memory addresses, unless you decide to go low level.

1.4.2 Lists

Lists differ a bit from the arrays in their implementation and also on how they lay on the main memory. For starters, let's call *node* each element from the list (similar to the *bucket* in the arrays).

Unlike arrays, lists are not necessarily made of contiguous memory locations. Actually, each node of the list holds a value and a *pointer* to the next node. The pointer is a memory address of the next element in the list, which is why lists are often called linked lists, since the nodes are linked.

The value can be of whatever data type you want to store (for example *8-bit* or *16-bit* integers as in the arrays, or some more complex *data types*). This means that the value part of the node will take enough memory locations to allocate the data type you are storing, whereas the pointer part of the node will occupy as many memory locations as needed to store memory addresses.

In the example above, the list is *singly linked*, meaning that each node only has one link (usually to the next node in the list). Linked lists can also be *doubly linked*, which means that each node has a pointer to the next and to the previous node in the list. As you can already conclude, the first element of the list (called the *head* of the list) doesn't have a *previous* pointer and the last element of the list doesn't have a *next* pointer. The last element of a list is not called the *tail*, as one would probably think. The *tail* actually refers to the list excluding its head.

1.4.3 Hash Tables, dictionaries and associative arrays

A **dictionary**, also known as an **associative array**, is a data structure that maps *keys* to *values*. A **Hash table** is a common implementation of such data structure.

Actually, a typical dictionary (English - English or English - Portuguese or whatever) is a physical representation of this abstraction: the *key* is the word and the *value* is its meaning, even though in computing the *value* can be (almost always) of any *type*.

Every possible *key* in a dictionary should occur only once. Hash tables implement dictionaries using a *hash function* to compute an index into an array bucket, and from there extract the desired value. A *hash function* is a function that receives an input (the *key*) and returns an output (the *hash*). This hash is then used to calculate the index of a bucket in an array where the *values* are stored. Ideally two different keys should have different hashes, means that if *F* is a hash function and *U* and *V* are two different keys, then the respective hashes should be different.

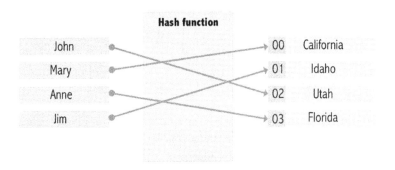

Nonetheless, this is not always the case. There are situations when two different keys compute the same hash, causing *collisions*. Actually, most hash table designs assume that hash collisions are an inevitability. As such, most implementations you'll come across have a strategy for collision resolution.

There are several strategies, but I will only briefly speak about one of them, even though chances are that in general you won't have to worry about this. Unless there is some very strong motive, you won't have to implement your own hash table.

The strategy is called *separate chaining*. When using *separate chaining*, each array bucket will hold a list of all the entries whose hash computed the same index. This means that the cost (in time) of search or insertion operation in hash tables that implement this kind of strategy is the cost of finding the right bucket (by computing the index from the hash of the key), which is constant, plus the cost of the list operation, which is *linear*. It's *linear* because it grows with the size of the list in a *linear* fashion.

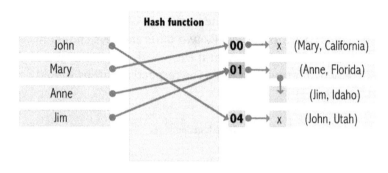

1.4.4 Sets

If you remember **sets** from your Math classes, then this data structure implements the finite sets you have learned. If you don't remember or haven't heard of, that's not an issue. A set is a container that stores values in no particular order and with the particularity of not allowing duplicates.

Certain languages, like Python, also implement static or frozen sets, which are immutable sets. This means that their contents cannot be changed after their creation. The range of operations you can perform on frozen sets is a bit more limited, since you can't change their contents. As such, you are restricted to query operations, like checking whether an element belongs to the set or not, checking the size of the set, getting the intersection or union between sets, and so on.

Since sets are unordered collections of elements, you cannot use indexes like you use in arrays to refer to an element in a certain position.

1.4.5 Trees

Last, but not least, there is the **tree** data structure. You are already familiar with this data structure, even though in a slightly different way: the family tree. The family tree is made up of nodes (the family members) and edges, which connect nodes to nodes or relationships between nodes to other nodes.

The **tree** data structure is a graph (a bunch of nodes and edges connecting the nodes, with some interesting properties) with a few restrictions: *it mustn't have cycles* and also *mustn't have disconnected parts*. As a consequence, you cannot have a child node with more than one parent. The trees vary in branching factor, which is the number of children each node has. Some trees are made of nodes that have at most two children: these are called *binary trees*. In "tree language" you'll often read or use certain terms. Here are a few examples:

- *Root*, which is the top node of the tree. Unlike the perennial plant, you often represent the tree data structure with its root at the top.
- *Child node*, a node directly connected to another, when you are traversing the tree downwards (away from the root)
- *Siblings*, which are obviously nodes with the same parent.
- *Leaf*, a node without children.

If you want to know all the terms used as well as expand your knowledge about tree data structure you should start with the Wikipedia's article *Tree data structure* [2].

Trees are the perfect data structure when you want to represent hierarchical data. A common use case is to represent the file hierarchy in certain file systems.

Trees are also suitable for storing data that needs to be efficiently searchable. An example of such data structure is the *binary search tree* (or *ordered tree*).

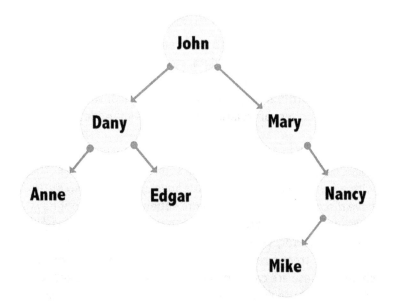

In the example above, each node contains a value (a string) and pointers for at most two children (hence the *binary tree*). You may also notice how the nodes are organized: for every node, the *subtree* that has its left child as root will only contain words lexicographically smaller and the *subtree* that has its right child as root will only contain words lexicographically greater. Take the node with the word Dany, for example. Its left subtree (which only has one node) only contains words lexicographically smaller (Anne, in this case). The same goes for the node John: every element to the left is smaller, whereas every element to the right is greater. This makes it very convenient to search, because you will never have to go through all the elements of the tree. The search starts in the root node (John). If you are looking for Edgar, the algorithm is quite simple: is Edgar equal to the value in the current node (John)? No. Is it greater? No. Is it smaller? Yes, then continue to the **left**. Is it equal to the value in the current node (Dany)?

No. Is it greater? Yes, then go to the **right**. Is it equal to the value in the current node (Edgar)? Yes, you've **found** it!

1.5 Algorithms

Algorithms and Data Structures are at the core of computer programming. An algorithm is like the steps in a recipe, a self-contained set of instructions and operations to be performed.

If the algorithm is the set of steps in a recipe, the data structures are the pots and bowls and whatever you use to store and mix your ingredients. Just like you have a bunch of recipes for all sorts of food, you also have a myriad of algorithms for all sort of purposes: searching, merging, inserting, deleting, sorting, slicing, matching data, you name it!

Some algorithms are more complex than others, and the type of data or data structure they are acting on also determines the *complexity* of the algorithm. The complexity of an algorithm is usually measured in terms of space and time.

This is what's called **analysis of algorithms**, in computer science: determining the amount of resources that the execution of an algorithm takes, measured in time and storage space. This is extremely important in determining the efficiency of an algorithm for solving a certain problem, as certain algorithms from the same class are more time efficient than others, whereas some others may be more space efficient.

Even though algorithms are at the core of computer programming, I won't be expanding this topic much further for two reasons: 1-) I would need an entire book to cover Algorithms (and there are already plenty of them out there, that do the job much better than I would do), and 2-) you don't need to possess detailed knowledge of algorithms and complexity in order to kick off.

You will, though, write your own algorithms more often than not: sequences of steps to manipulate data that your program will deal with. They may not be the most efficient at the beginning, but as you gain experience, you'll be able to write either shorter or faster algorithms (or both) that will take less storage space to accomplish the same.

1.6 Computer Networking

Depending on the nature of the software you write, most likely you will write applications with several communicating parts, spread across more than one network.

You will probably be using some 3rd party API to enrich your application. More often than not, applications allow users to log in using their Facebook or Google+ credentials. Perhaps you want to collect data from tweets in order to find some weird pattern, and for that you would probably use Twitter's API.

All of this is possible because of this giant computer network called Internet: billions of devices interconnected, where some of them are service providers, others are consumers, others are both. It's a network made up of collections of networks and nobody owns it.

I won't go into details about how things work behind the scenes, but I will introduce you to the most important concepts by giving you an idea of what happens when you type "www.google.com" in your browser's address bar and hit the "Enter" key.

1.6.1 IP Address, localhost and port

The first thing that you need to know is that every single device that is connected to the Internet has a unique identifier, which is called the *IP Address*.

The version of the IP Address that is most widely used is called IPv4, which defines IP Addresses as being a *32-bit* integer. By the time that IPv4 was created (back in 1981), it was more than enough, since with 32 bits you can represent up to 4.3 billion (or 2^{32}) unique values. Or 4,294,967,296 to be more precise. Well, so it happens that this number is no longer sufficient to cover all the devices connected to the internet... Actually this limitation was taken into consideration 26 years ago, when the development of IPv6 began (in 1990). IPv6 addresses, on the other hand, are represented by *128-bit* integers, which means that it supports 2^{128} (or 3.4×10^{38}) unique IP addresses. It's quite a lot.

A typical IPv4 address looks like this: **209.85.202.99**. The same IP address using v6 is **0:0:0:0:0:ffff:d155:ca63**. I told you that an IPv4 address is a *32-bit* integer, so how come it's represented as **209.85.202.99**? Ok, let's recall what you've learned about binary numeral system. With 8 bits you can represent up to 256 different integers (usually from 0 to 255). The IP address above has 4 different parts separated by dots. And you are correct when you conclude, my clever reader, that each part ranges from 0 to 255, meaning that in theory IPv4 addresses range from 0.0.0.0 to 255.255.255.255. Each part is called an *octet*.

Let's put this aside for a bit and go back to the point where I told you that each device connected to the Internet has a unique IP Address assigned. Well, sort of...

Let's say that you are at home with your laptop connected to the Internet. You also have your smartphone connected and the same goes for your wife, husband, boyfriend, girlfriend, whoever you live with. You are all connected to the fancy *router* that was installed by your Internet Service Provider (ISP).

In fact, your devices aren't connected directly to the Internet, they are behind your home router, which in turn will connect to the routers of your ISP (with a few hops in between, but they don't matter for now). This means that your home router *is* the device connected to the Internet and has the unique IP Address.

What about your computer? And your smartphone? Well, your home router assigns IP Addresses to all the devices connected to it, but they are only used for internal purposes. They are only used in the scope of your home network, also known as LAN (or *Local Area Network*) or WLAN (*Wireless Local Area Network*). These are called *private IP addresses*, since they are only used in the scope of a private network.

Don't worry if things are still a bit unclear to you. Soon this will all make sense, I promise! Let's review what you know so far:

- Every single device that is connected to the Internet has a unique IP Address assigned.
- An IP Address is a *32-bit* integer, in case of IPv4 (which is the most widely used standard). In case of IPv6, it's a *128-bit* integer. We'll focus on the former for now.
- In the scenario of a home network, your router is the device connected to the Internet. It has a unique IP Address that was assigned by your ISP.
- The router assigns private IP Addresses to every device connected to it (your smartphone, your laptop, your printer, etc). These IP Addresses are used in the scope of your private network.

Good! Now, the router keeps some sort of configuration table that maps unique private IP Addresses to the devices connected to it. At the moment, I have 2 devices connected to my home router: my laptop and my smartphone. My laptop was assigned the private IP Address 192.168.2.2 and my smartphone 192.168.2.3. The first 3 octets identify the *network* (192.168.2) and the last octet identifies the *host* inside that network. So my laptop is host 2 in the network 192.168.2.

These private IP Addresses are only unique in your home network, behind your router. It is possible for someone in another country to be with his laptop connected to his home router and have the same private IP Address as me! But the router connected to the ISP will have a unique public IP Address.

Now let's say that I'm on my laptop with my browser open and I type "www.google.com" in the address bar and hit "Enter". My browser is sending this request to the router, the router forwards the request to the ISP routers, gets a response back and *routes* it to the correct device: my laptop. It does so because it knows that the response that it gets comes from a request that is associated to a certain private IP Address. And according to its configuration table, that private IP Address is associated to my laptop. Easy peasy, right?

On a side note, you will often see the IP address **127.0.0.1**, also referred to as *localhost*. This is the IP address used to establish an IP connection to the same local machine (or computer) used by the end-user. So, if you try to connect to 127.0.0.1 from your computer, you are actually trying to connect to a service running in your computer... But which service? Services (provided by programs or processes) are identified by a *port*, which is a *16-bit* integer. **If the IP address identifies a computer in a network, the *port* identifies a service running in that computer**. Since a *port* is identified by a *16-bit* integer, you have up to 65536 ports available.

Imagine a building, let's say the City Hall in the city where you live. In this building, there are several departments, for example Taxes departments, Immigration department, Social Security, whatever. Each of these services is running in a specific room. The building itself is identified by its public IP address and this building represents a computer and the Operating System running in it. The different ports identify the different services running inside the building.

So let's say that you, a citizen (the *client*), want to go to the Taxes department. You know the IP address of the City Hall and go there with whatever request you have. There is a doorman, who knows about all the services running in that building and which port identifies them. This doorman's name is Kernel. You go to him and say "Excuse me, Mr. Kernel, I have a request for a service running on port 1234 in this building identified by this IP address". And Kernel says "Oh yes, that is the Taxes department. Give me the request, I'll bring you the response right away". You just established a connection with the City Hall and its Taxes department and you are now waiting for a response. The Kernel brings the response and you leave. Now let's suppose that later you come back with another request, for a non-existent service, mentioning port 9872. This time the Kernel says "My apologies, sir, I must refuse your request to connect because we don't have such service". Ooops!

Someone now decides to build another service, a Fire department, and have it running in the City Hall. The people who built that service (who wrote that software) decided that they want it to be open to the general public and will be listening for new connections on port 6798. Of course, they made Mr. Kernel aware of it, so that he can forward the requests to the correct service when someone needs to use the Fire department, instead of refusing connections.

Sometimes, some departments need to use the City Hall's internal services. The Police department needed to use the Immigration department's service, which was identified by port 5201. This time, because it's an internal service, Mr.

Kernel can be reached by the internal IP address of the City Hall: **127.0.0.1**. Whenever a service in the City Hall acts like a *client* and tries to establish a connection to another service using the IP address **127.0.0.1**, that request goes to a service inside that building (or computer, or machine). Of course, the services need to be accepting connections, or else Mr. Kernel will still refuse, even if the request comes from an internal service.

The *localhost*, or **127.0.0.1**, is like the word "me". When I say "me", I'm referring to myself. If you say "me", you are referring to yourself. If a software in a computer tries to connect to a service using the IP 127.0.0.1, it means that it's trying to connect to a service running in that same computer, in that local machine.

Now that you have a basic understanding, let me introduce a new layer of complexity. I told you that each device connected to the Internet is assigned a unique IP Address, which means that the Google servers connected to the Internet should have unique IP Addresses, right? Right. So how come you write "www.google.com" in the address bar of your browser? Well, because that's far easier to remember than 209.85.202.99. So in that case, if it's the IP Address that uniquely identifies a device and we are providing a name... how does the request arrive at the right place? Or at the right server, in this case?

1.6.2 DNS

This is where **DNS** comes into play. DNS (*Domain Name System*) is a hierarchy of decentralized naming systems for any device connected to any network, public (Internet) or private. One of the most important services that DNS provides is the translation between domain names and IP Addresses.

So how is DNS used when you are surfing the web and hitting Google homepage as specified in the previous example? In first place, the browser will check for the domain name in its cache. Most likely it will find it there, but in case it doesn't then it contacts a DNS server and makes a query: what is the IP Address for the domain name "google.com"? How does it know which DNS server to contact? When you connect your laptop to your home router, not only it will assign a private IP Address to your laptop as it will also provide the IP Address of one or more DNS servers (this information is provided by your ISP). You can also configure manually which DNS server to use, but that's irrelevant for now.

So here's a short summary of what happens when you want to go to "www.google.com":

- Your browser checks for the domain name in its cache.
- If it exists in cache, then it will grab the IP Address and "tell" your home router: Hey, could you please perform a request on this IP Address?
- If it doesn't exist in cache, then it will ask your home router to query a DNS server about the IP Address of google.com
- The DNS server responds with the IP Address and your home router forwards the response to your computer. Afterwards, the browser forwards the request to that IP Address to your home router and it will take care of the rest.

Skipping tremendous amounts of details and complexity, of course. But this is the main idea, so if you understand this it's already good enough.

1.6.3 Network Protocols (HTTP, HTTPS and beyond)

As I mentioned earlier in the **IP Address** section, a protocol is a pre-defined way of speaking with a service. When you are accessing "www.google.com", your browser is going to speak HTTP with the server at the IP Address associated with the name google.com. That server is running a service that serves the web page to clients using HTTP protocol. In fact, nowadays your browser speaks HTTPS instead of HTTP when you access www.google.com. HTTPS stands for HTTP Secure and it adds a security layer on top of HTTP protocol (meaning that in theory your communications using HTTPS protocol are secure).

Another widely used protocol is SMTP, which stands for Simple Mail Transfer Protocol, and is the one spoken when you are accessing your email using some email clients (like Mail on Mac OS X, Outlook on Windows, etc).

If you are curious about these (and other protocols), I would recommend you reading thoroughly this Wikipedia entry about *Application Layer Protocols*[3]. The name "Application Layer" already gives away the fact that there ARE other Layers. If you take a look at the box on the right side of the Wikipedia entry, you will notice a title saying "Internet protocol suite" and four layers: Application Layer, Transport Layer, Internet Layer and Link Layer. They show up in a specific order for a reason. Go ahead, start exploring this by clicking on "Internet protocol suite"! I promise the ride will be fun!

--- ◆ ---

Summary

What you've learned in this chapter:

- Main memory (**RAM**) is a volatile storage, which means that all the data will be lost when you restart your computer.
- RAM can be seen as a bunch of sequence numbered Gym lockers, where each locker is a storage location with fixed size: 1 byte.
- **1 byte = 8 bits**. You can represent 2 values with 1 bit (0 and 1), 4 values with 2 bits (00, 01, 10 and 11) and 2Nvalues with N bits. 1 byte can represent up to 256 different values (ranging from 0 to 255).

- **Data Structures** are used to store and organize data in a particular way. Examples of data structures are: **Arrays**, **Lists**, **Hash Tables** (an implementation of **Dictionaries**), **Sets** and **Trees**.
- Every device that is connected to the **Internet** is assigned a unique identifier called **IP Address**.
- The two main norms for the IP Address are **IPv4** (which is a *32-bit* integer) and **IPv6** (a *128-bit* integer).
- When connecting to the Internet through a router, a device is assigned a **private IP Address**, which is only used in the scope of the private network.
- **DNS** servers are responsible for translating domain names into IP Addresses.

Step 2 – Jumping head first into Python

If you've made it this far, congratulations! Unless you were already acquainted with the concepts presented in the previous step, I hope you haven't skipped it! Here is what you'll have learned by the end of Step 2:

- How to use Python **interactive shell** to write and test code on the fly
- Python's main **data types** and **operators**
- What **Character Encoding** is
- Difference between **ASCII** and **UTF-8**
- How to control the **flow** of execution in your programs
- Write and use **functions**
- Access and modify **files**
- Handle **errors** and **exceptions** in your programs
- Work with **modules** to enrich your applications
- Main concepts of **Object Oriented** and **Functional** programming **paradigms**
- Have a good understanding of the underlying idea behind generators and iterators.

Python is an interpreted high-level programming language. It's called interpreted because there is a special software (the Python interpreter) that interprets whatever Python code you write and produces a result (if it didn't find any error). In general, Python allows you to clearly express concepts in fewer lines of code than languages like Java or C++. It supports multiple programming paradigms, such as object-oriented, imperative and functional. We'll see later what these programming paradigms are. When you run a program written in Python, you do so by using a Python interpreter. Python, by itself, is just a language: nothing more than a specification with rules about vocabulary, syntax, semantics, etc. An interpreter is an implementation of that specification. The most widely used (and the one used throughout this book) is called CPython, which is an implementation (written in C language) that contains all the new features and bug fixes.

> **Note**: new versions of the language follow the nomenclature `major.minor.micro` for releases ready for production. This means that for Python 3.5.1 its major version is 3, the minor version is 5 and the micro version is 1. Major versions are the least frequent and only happen when changes that break compatibility are really necessary. The minor versions happen when new features are introduced and usually take place every 18 months. The micro versions are mainly for bug fixes and happen every 6 months (or a bit more frequently, if necessary). Python has two major versions: 2 and 3. Even though it's recommended for newcomers to adopt Python 3, many developers are still using Python 2, either because upgrading would break compatibility with current code or because certain libraries are still not available for Python 3. This has may also have some consequences for you as a developer, because more often than not you will need to use external libraries in your application and they may not be compatible with your current version of Python.

The Python interpreter can be used in a few different ways, but in this book we will just use two of them:

- You can just invoke it on the *command line* and use it in interactive mode. This means that the interpreter will read and execute interactively the commands you type.
- You can invoke it in the command line and provide a filename as an argument, in order to execute the *script* from the file.

2.1 Your first interaction with Python: the interactive shell

If you work on Mac OS X, you already have version 2 of Python installed. The same goes for certain Linux distributions (Ubuntu also should have Python 2 and 3 installed by default).

Unfortunately, Windows doesn't come with any version of Python. Nonetheless, like I said before, you should be using Python 3, especially if you're a newcomer. So the first thing you should do is to install the latest version of Python 3. Just head to the *download*[4] section in the official website and download the version 3.5.2 for your operating system. The installation is quite straightforward.

Let's start our adventures in Python by invoking the interpreter in interactive mode: type *python* and hit the *Enter* key. Sometimes, depending on the installation, you may have to invoke the command *python3* or *python3.5* instead, or else you will be running Python 2.

This is where we will run most of the examples in this chapter and also do some experiments in future chapters. It can also be used as a calculator, which is pretty awesome. When the interactive shell starts, it dumps some information which is not much relevant for you, except maybe for the version of Python that you are running. In my case, I'm running Python 3.5.2 (which is currently the latest stable version from the branch with major version 3). If your interpreter doesn't show a version 3.5.* then you should start it with the proper command, mentioned above. Exit the interpreter by typing **quit()** and hitting *Enter* and restart it in the correct way.

If you want to use it as a calculator, all you have to do is type the expression and hit Enter:

```
>>> 2 + 2
4
>>> 3 * 2
6
>>> 25 / 5
5.0
>>> 2 + 3 * 2
8
```

2.2 Data Types

In the previous example, you entered *expressions* and the interpreter evaluated them. Those expressions produced a *value* and values have *types*. To check the type of a value, you can use the *built-in function* **type** and pass the value as an *argument* to the function, with parentheses surrounding it. Some functions don't expect any argument and you've already used such function: **quit**. When you invoke a function that doesn't expect any argument, you just call it by writing its name followed by (). We'll explore functions in more detail later, for now let's stick to the types.

2.2.1 Numbers

```
>>> type(4)
<class 'int'>
```

The value 4 has type *int*, which represents positive and negative Integers in an unlimited range, as you learned in Math. Actually, there are two types of integers in Python: *int* and *bool* (Boolean), with values True and False. Boolean is a subtype of integer and its two only values behave like the integer values 1 and 0, respectively, in almost all contexts.

```
>>> type(True)
<class 'bool'>
>>> type(False)
<class 'bool'>
```

Booleans represent the relationship between a proposition and truth. Such as:

```
>>> 1 > 2
False
```

```
>>> 1 + 1 == 2
True
>>> type(1) is int
True
>>> type(1) is float
False
```

Note the **==** in the second expression. This is a comparison operator and compares the values of two *objects*. The objects don't need to be of the same type. In this situation, you are comparing the result of 1 + 1 with 2. The operator **is** compares the identity of two objects. In both cases it compares the result of invoking **type(1)** with whatever you put on the right hand side. When you invoke **type(1)**, the result is the type of the value 1, which is *int*. Don't worry if this still feels a bit confusing for you. As you continue reading, things will become more clear and I'll make sure to cover these points more than once.

What about 5.0?

```
>>> type(5.0)
<class 'float'>
```

The value 5.0 has type *float* (Real Number). Just like *int*, *float* is also a *numeric type* in Python.

Note: float numbers precision in Python are limited by the underlying machine architecture. You should read *Floating Point Arithmetics: Issues and Limitations*[5] section of Python's tutorial to have a better understanding about what to expect and what problems you may face.

Python supports a third numeric type called *complex*, which represents Complex numbers with double precision floating point numbers. It uses the suffix j or J to indicate the imaginary part:

```
>>> type(3 + 2j)
<class 'complex'>
```

2.2.1.2 Numeric Operators

The following table contains some of the operations supported by all numeric types, except for complex. If you wish to see the full list of operations consult *Built-in Types*[6] chapter from *Python Standard Library*.

Operation	Result
x + y	Addition
x - y	Subtraction
x * y	Multiplication
x / y	Division
x // y	Integer division (the quotient between x and y will be floored)
x % y	Modulo (the remainder after the division between x and y)
-x	x negated
int(x)	Converts x to an integer.
float(x)	Converts x to floating point
pow(x, y)	x to the power y
x**y	x to the power y

(*Numeric operators*)

You can also perform the following bitwise operations over Integers (they only make sense for integers, not for other types):

Operation	Result
x | y	Bitwise x **OR** y
x & y	Bitwise x **AND** y
x^y	Bitwise x **XOR** y
x << n	x shifted *n* bits to the left
x >> n	x shifted *n* bits to the right
~x	Bitwise **NOT** x

(*Bitwise Operators*)

2.2.2 Sequences

In the section *Data Structures* from Step 1 you already made acquaintance with some *sequence* types, such as Arrays and Lists. *Sequences* represent ordered collections with a finite number of elements, that can be *indexed* by integers. They can be *mutable* (Lists and ByteArrays) or *immutable* (Strings, Tuples and Bytes). Immutable sequences cannot change after their creation, whereas mutable sequences can. Nonetheless, it's possible that an immutable sequence is made of mutable objects, which means that the elements of the sequence can change.

2.2.2.1 Strings
A string (*str*) is a sequence of characters and can be enclosed by a pair of single quotes, a pair of double quotes or a pair of triple quotes (both """ and ''').

```
>>> type('This is a string')
<class 'str'>
>>> type("This is also a string")
```

```
<class 'str'>
>>> type('''So is this one''')
<class 'str'>
>>> type("""Or even this one""")
<class 'str'>
```

Variables

A "little" side note: So far we've used the values directly, making things as interesting as an empty bottle of milk. Let's spice up a bit by using *variables*. A *variable* is a binding between a name and an object of whatever data type. You assign a value to a variable using the *assignment* (**=**) operator between the name of the variable (on the left side) and the value (on the right side). Don't mix this with == operator, which compares the values of two objects.

```
>>> my_age = 34
>>> type(my_age)
<class 'int'>
>>> my_name = "Pedro"
>>> type(my_name)
<class 'str'>
```

In this example, we assigned the value 34 to the variable *my_age* and, as you can see, the type of the variable is *int*. On the other hand, the variable *my_name* has type *str* (short for string), since it was assigned a string as a value. If you just write the name of the variable and hit Enter, its value will be printed:

```
>>> my_age
34
```

If you refer to the name of a variable that wasn't previously defined, the interpreter will complain by saying that the name wasn't defined:

```
>>> your_age
Traceback (most recent call last):
  File "<stdin>", line 1, in <module>
NameError: name 'your_age' is not defined
```

You can also assign expressions to variables, such as:

```
>>> x = 1
>>> y = 2
>>> z = x + y
>>> z
3
```

Throughout the book, we'll do some more complex stuff with variables, for now I'm just whetting your appetite!

There are some restrictions on the naming convention for variables, such as:

- A variable's name can only contain the letters from the alphabet (lower and uppercase), underscores and digits, as long as digits are not the first character:

```
>>> my age = 34
  File "<stdin>", line 1
    my age = 34
         ^
SyntaxError: invalid syntax
>>> my_age123 = 34
>>> my_age123
34
>>> 123my_age = 34
  File "<stdin>", line 1
    123my_age = 34
           ^
SyntaxError: invalid syntax
```

- Variables names are case sensitive, which means that my_age and My_age are different variables. You should be careful with this and try to be consistent when it comes to naming your variables. Actually, the best is for you to follow *PEP8*[7], which is a guide for Python coding style.

```
>>> my_age = 34
>>> My_age = 12
>>> my_age
34
>>> My_age
12
```

- You can't use as name for a variable any of Python's keywords (reserved words of the language itself):

False	Class	finally	is	return
None	continue	for	lambda	try
True	def	from	nonlocal	while
and	del	global	not	with
as	elif	if	or	yield
assert	else	import	pass	
break	except	in	raise	

(*Python's reserved words*)

A good rule of thumb for naming your variables is to give them self-explanatory nouns as names and use underscores to separate words. Just don't go crazy and call a variable `this_is_my_age` when it could simply be called `my_age`.

A last note is that you don't need to tell the interpreter what is the type of your variable: it immediately assumes, depending on the value you are assigning to it. That's why Python is a dynamically typed language, since the type of a variable will be determined on runtime (when the interpreter is running your program).

Now back to the *string* data type! Depending on which quotes you are using to enclose your string, you may have to *escape* some characters. Let's see an example with a single quoted string:

```
>>> example = 'I'm going home.'
  File "<stdin>", line 1
    example = 'I'm going home.'
                ^
SyntaxError: invalid syntax
```

Did you understand what happened? Basically, when I wrote `I'm`, the interpreter assumed that the quote was a string delimiter, which means that what followed the string "`I`" was invalid, hence the syntax error. Since we don't want the interpreter to assume that the quote in `I'm` is a string delimiter, we must *escape* that character:

```
>>> example = 'I\'m going home.'
>>> example
"I'm going home."
```

An escape character invokes an alternative interpretation and in Python you escape with a backslash (\). Oh, and don't be confused with the double quotes on line 3, the interpreter delimits strings either with single or double quotes when it prints them.

Certain characters have a special meaning when escaped. For example, if you escape a lower case `n`, then you are inserting a *newline* character in the string (\n):

```
>>> example = "This is one line.\nThis is another
line."
>>> example
```

```
'This is one line.\nThis is another line.'
>>> print(example)
This is one line.
This is another line.
```

You don't even need to separate the *n* from the *T*. When you enter the variable name and hit Enter key, you are shown its actual value. Only when you print the string (by invoking the **print** function and passing the string as argument), the *newline* character is actually interpreted as a newline and the string is split at the place where it occurred. There are other escape characters, like the \t for tab:

```
>>> example = "String with a\ttab"
>>> example
'String with a\ttab'
>>> print(example)
String with a    tab
```

What if, for some reason, you want to write a string with a backslash preceding the consonant *n* but you don't want it to be interpreted as a newline? Then in that case you must escape the backslash:

```
>>> example = "This is \\not a \\newline"
>>> example
'This is \\not a \\newline'
>>> print(example)
This is \not a \newline
```

Now let's play a bit with triple quoted strings. Triple quoted strings are useful when you want to write a string that spans several lines. Watch this:

```
>>> example = """
... This is a string that
... spans more than two lines. It's cool
... just to understand how it
```

```
... works"""
>>> example
"\nThis is a string that\nspans more than two lines.
It's cool\njust to understand how it\nworks\n"
>>> print(example)

This is a string that
spans more than two lines. It's cool
just to understand how it
works
```

Notice how the escape characters for new lines were automatically placed in the string. Also, when you are writing a statement in the interactive shell that should span more than one line, the shell automatically starts the next line with three dots (. . .). Triple quoted strings are also used when writing comments in your code. Further down the road, you'll see it in use.

As I said before, strings are immutable sequences, which means that once they are created, they cannot be changed:

```
>>> example = "Hello, world!"
>>> example[0]
'H'
>>> example[1]
'e'
>>> example[2]
'l'
>>> example[2] = "r"
Traceback (most recent call last):
  File "<stdin>", line 1, in <module>
TypeError: 'str' object does not support item
assignment
```

Confused with the first few lines? Let me refresh your memory: a string is a sequence type, which means that you can *index* its elements with integer numbers. Do you remember the *Array* data type? You could index them with square brackets and an integer (called *subscript*), where 0 refers to the first element and *n - 1* refers to the last element (*n* being the number of elements in the Array). In the above example, we are indexing the first (0), second (1) and third (2) characters of the string. On the next line, we are trying to replace the third character of the string with r, but the interpreter complains, because strings are *immutable*.

And can we refer to more than one character of the string at once? For example, get a *substring*? Of course we can, we can use something called *slicing*. When you *slice* a sequence type, you do so by specifying the beginning of the slice, the end of the slice (which is an index not included in the slice) and the step.

We'll see in a bit what the step is. Let's examine the following example:

```
>>> example[2:10]
'llo, wor'
```

In this example, our *substring* starts on index 2 of the string stored in the variable *example* and it ends at the index 10, BUT the character at index 10 is not included. As a matter of fact, you can create a slice without specifying its beginning, like this:

```
>>> example[:10]
'Hello, wor'
```

If you don't specify the beginning, then index 0 is automatically assumed. The same goes for the end of the slice: if you don't specify it, then the length of the string is assumed.

```
>>> example[3:]
'lo, world!'
```

Can we use negative indexes? Of course we can! With negative indexes, you reference the string backwards. Since there is no negative zero, the last character of the string is indexed with −1, the character before that is indexed with −2 and so on. The first character has the negative index -*n*, where *n* is the length of the string:

```
>>> example[-1]
'!'
>>> example[-2]
'd'
>>> example[-13]
'H'
```

We can also slice with negative indexes:

```
>>> example[-12:-5]
'ello, w'
```

What if we inverted the negative indexes in the slice, what would be the result?

```
>>> example[-5:-12]
''
```

An empty string? How's that? Well, this is my cue to introduce the *step* of a slice. When omitted, the step is 1 by default. What does this mean? It means that you will get a slice of the original string by advancing 1 character at a time. Which means that if you specify a slice [i:j] (the same as [i:j:1]) then the first element of the slice starts on the index i, the second element is indexed by i+1, the third element indexed by i+2, and so on. The index of the next character is retrieved by adding the step to the index of the current character. If you define a step 2, then your result will be slightly different:

```
>>> example[2:10]
'llo, wor'
```

```
>>> example[2:10:2]
'lo o'
```

On the first slice, the *step* is omitted which means that it's 1, so the slicing advances 1 character at a time. On the second example, the slicing advances 2 characters at a time, resulting in a slightly different substring. And you may be wondering, dear reader, if the step can be a negative integer. Indeed, it can! This is how you solve the empty string with inverted negative indexes:

```
>>> example[-5:-14:-1]
'ow ,olleH'
```

Since the step is added to the index of the previous character, you get a slice in reverse. The first character has index -5; the second character has index $-5 + (-1)$, which is -6; the third character has index $-6 + (-1)$, which is -7; and so on.

Let's see how can you use slices to create a copy of a string (or any sequence type):

```
>>> example[:]
'Hello, world!'
```

Remember that if you don't specify the beginning of the slice, then the index 0 (the first character of the string) is assumed by default. And if you don't specify the end of the slice, then *n* (where *n* is the number of characters of the string, or its length) is assumed. As a matter of fact, this creates a *shallow copy* of the string. In Python, you have two copy operations: *shallow* and *deep*. I will explain later the difference between both.

And now, the million-dollar question: how do you reverse a string using slicing? Meaning, how can you obtain the string

`!dlrow ,olleH` by slicing the string `Hello, world!`? I'll let you think for a bit, before giving you a possible solution. **Hint**: you can slice just by specifying the step and omitting the beginning and the end of the slice (as in `[::step]`).

There are many other things you can do with strings. For starters, you can check its *length* (and of any other sequence type) by using the built-in function **len**:

```
>>> len("Hello, world!")
13
>>> example = "Hello, world!"
>>> len(example)
13
```

You can also *concatenate* two or more strings, using the **+** operator. Note that if you use this operator with numbers, then the arithmetic addition operation will take place, but if you use it with two strings (or other sequences), then they will be concatenated. This is possible due to *operator overloading*, which is a feature of the language that allows you to redefine the behavior of operators, depending on the type of arguments being used. We'll see more into this later.

```
>>> "Hello, world!" + "How are you?"
'Hello, world!How are you?'
>>> string1 = "Hello, world!"
>>> string2 = "How are you?"
>>> string3 = string1 + string2
>>> string3
'Hello, world!How are you?'
>>> string1[:7] + "Pedro!"
'Hello, Pedro!'
```

Thanks to operator overloading, you can also repeat a string as many times as you want using the multiplication operator *****:

```
>>> "Hello, world!" * 2
'Hello, world!Hello, world!'
>>> 2 * "Hello, world!"
'Hello, world!Hello, world!'
>>> "Hello, world!" * 4
'Hello, world!Hello, world!Hello, world!Hello, world!'
>>> "Hello, world!" * 0
''
```

Note: make sure you check Python's official documentation in order to have a full coverage of everything you can do with strings (and other data types): *Text Sequence Types - str*[8]. Actually, the official documentation should be one of your best friends.

Enough of strings for now!

2.2.2.2 Tuples

Tuples are another immutable sequence type that can be useful to store immutable ordered collections of homogeneous or heterogeneous data. A tuple can have an arbitrary number of elements, including zero, and you can build them in several different ways:

```
>>> x = ()  # A pair of parentheses denotes an empty
⌐tuple
>>> x
()
>>> type(x)
<class 'tuple'>
>>> x = 1,  # A trailing comma for creating a tuple
⌐with one element
>>> x
(1,)
>>> x = (1,) # A trailing comma for creating a tuple
⌐with one element
>>> x
(1,)
>>> x = 1, 2, 3  # Separating elements with commas
>>> x
(1, 2, 3)
>>> x = (1, 2, 3)  # Separating elements with commas
```

```
>>> x
(1, 2, 3)
```

Note: I also took the chance to introduce you to something that is crucial when writing software: **comments**. I even wrote the word comments in bold so that you understand how important they are. Comments allow you to write annotations on your code in order to make it more understandable, not just for you but also for whoever reads your code or works on it. They are ignored by the interpreter, so whenever it detects a **#**, it ignores whatever comes after (on the same line). Unless, of course, the # occurs inside a string, on which case it's treated as a character of the string. Avoid comments that don't bring any value or that state the obvious. Don't forget that, at the end of the day, your code should be clear and self-explanatory! Here are a couple of examples of useless comments, due to stating the obvious:

```
>>> x = y + 1   # x is y plus one
>>> reversed = string[::-1]   # Reverses the string
```

Last, but not least, you can build a tuple from an *iterable*, just like this:

```
>>> t = tuple("Hello, world!")
>>> t
('H', 'e', 'l', 'l', 'o', ',', ' ', 'w', 'o', 'r', 'l', 'd', '!')
```

What the hell is an *iterable*? Well, an *iterable* is an object that has the capability of returning its elements one at a time. It does so using an *iterator*, which is an object that represents a stream of data. The sequence type *string*, for example, is an *iterable* because you can retrieve its characters one at a time using an iterator. We'll see more about *iterables* in the section **Control Flow and Functions**, since they are often used in `for` loops. Lists, tuples and dictionaries are also *iterable* objects. This means that you can build a tuple from a tuple:

```
>>> t = (1, 2, 3)
>>> t
(1, 2, 3)
```

```
>>> w = tuple(t)
>>> w
(1, 2, 3)
```

A tuple can also have tuples as elements, and elements of different types:

```
>>> t = ((1, 2, 3), "Hello, world!", 2)
>>> t
((1, 2, 3), 'Hello, world!', 2)
```

In this example, tuple t has 3 elements: a *tuple*, a *string* and an *integer*. Since a tuple is a sequence type, you can access its elements with subscript:

```
>>> t[0]
(1, 2, 3)
>>> t[1]
'Hello, world!'
>>> t[1][0]
'H'
```

You may have noticed that, on my last command, I used subscript with two indices: t[1][0] . If you are familiar with the notion of matrix, then you probably understood what happened immediately. If not, this is actually quite simple: I am referencing the first element from the second element in the tuple (remember that the first element is indexed by 0, the second by 1, and so on). So, the second element from the tuple is t[1], which is the string "Hello, world!". The first element from the string, t[1][0], is the character H. We can create a tuple with more nested elements, so that you fully understand how this works:

```
>>> t = ((1, 2, 3), (("a", "b", "c"), "Hello, world!",
 ↵"d"), 2)
```

```
>>> t[1]
(('a', 'b', 'c'), 'Hello, world!', 'd')
>>> t[1][0]
('a', 'b', 'c')
>>> t[1][0][2]
'c'
```

The most confusing part is probably the amount of parentheses. When you use a text editor or a fancy IDE (Integrated Development Environment, which is a text editor on steroids), you will probably have highlighted the matching opening and closing parentheses.

2.2.2.3 Bytes

We've entered the last immutable sequence type: *bytes*. In Step 1 you learned what a byte is: 8 bits of data. You also know that with 1 byte you can represent 256 different integers, usually ranging from *0* to *255* (or *0 <= x < 256*). So a *bytes* object is an immutable sequence of individual bytes and only *ASCII characters* are allowed on byte literals.

Before explaining what *ASCII characters* are, I need to explain what *Character Encoding* is. In a nutshell, *Character Encoding* is a way of representing characters using an encoding system, which can be based on symbols, bit patterns, numbers, etc. Think of the Morse Code: it encodes letters from A to Z and digits from 0 to 9 using combinations of dots and dashes. Morse Code can be seen as an encoding system. In computing, you have a myriad of encoding systems and **ASCII** (*American Standard Code for Information Interchange*) is just one of them. ASCII uses integers from 0 to 127 to encode a total of 128 characters based on the English alphabet. There are other encoding systems that encode characters from other alphabets, like Cyrillic or Latin. Even though there are lots of encoding systems to encode different character sets, the truth is that this is far from being flexible, especially if you have a multi-lingual text, because some encodings are incompatible with others. To solve this and other problems, **Unicode** was created. **Unicode** is a standard, with the aim of representing and handling text expressed in most of the world's writing systems. Its latest version supports up to 120,000 characters. There are several encoding systems that implement the Unicode standard, and **UTF-8** is one of them. In fact, **UTF-8** dethroned ASCII, which used to be the most popular encoding system on the Web. UTF-8 is backwards compatible with ASCII, as it uses 1 byte to encode any ASCII character and up to 4 bytes to encode any other character. All the ASCII characters have the same code in ASCII and UTF-8.

Now that you are familiar with Character Encoding, let's go back to *bytes* data type. Like I said, bytes objects are an ordered sequence of individual bytes. Each byte of the sequence can only contain ASCII characters, which are represented by numbers between 0 and 127 (7 bits). But one single byte can represent up to 256 different integers, which means that if you want to store integers bigger than 127 in a bytes sequence they must be properly escaped.

Bytes sequences can be built in several different ways. For example, you can build them just as you build strings, the difference being that you need to add a *"b"* prefix.

```
>>> type(b"Hello, world!")
<class 'bytes'>
>>> type(b'Hello, world!')
<class 'bytes'>
>>> type(b'''Hello, world!''')
<class 'bytes'>
>>> type(b"""Hello, world!""")
<class 'bytes'>
```

These *bytes* sequences only contain ASCII characters. Let's confirm it! First, I would ask you to check the table of ASCII characters in the Appendix A. The table has 4 columns and each column has 4 sub-columns: Char, Dec, Oct, Hex. The first sub-column is the ASCII character. The other 3 sub-columns are the same integer represented in 3 numbering systems: Decimal, Octal and Hexadecimal. As you can see, the first character (nul) in the table is represented by the integer 0. The last character is represented by the integer 127 and is the character (del).

Bytes objects have a *method* called **hex**, which returns a hexadecimal representation of the *bytes* object.

> **Note**: a *method* is a term used in Object Oriented Programming and refers to a function associated to an object. In the section *2.8 Object Oriented Programming* I will explain in detail what this programming paradigm is about.

```
>>> x = b"Hello, world!"
>>> x
b'Hello, world!'
>>> x.hex()
'48656c6c6f2c20776f726c6421'
```

The result of invoking the method **hex** in the *bytes* object x is a string representing the hexadecimal value of that object. The . operator (*dot*) is used to either invoke the method of an object or to access a property of that object. But like I said, I'll tell you all about this later on.

Back to the bytes! Let's refresh your memory regarding hexadecimal numbering system: a hexadecimal number is made of 16 different symbols, where the first ten symbols are the digits from 0 to 9 (representing their integer values) and the remaining 6 are the letters **a**, **b**, **c**, **d**, **e** and **f**. The letters represent the integers 10, 11, 12, 13, 14 and 15 respectively.

Can you tell me the integer value of the hexadecimal number 3c? Right, it's 60: **3·16+12**. What about 4df? Yep, it's 1247: 4·16²+13·16+15. What about ff? It's 255. Which means that with 2 hexadecimal symbols you can represent up to 256 integers: from 0 (or 00 in hexadecimal) to 255 (or ff). You need exactly two hexadecimal symbols to represent 1 byte (8 bits) of data. As you may remember, a *bytes* object is a sequence of integers that range from 0 to 255. Which means that every two symbols in that hexadecimal representation of the *bytes* object actually represent one single byte of the sequence: an ASCII character:

```
48 65 6c 6c 6f 2c 20 77 6f 72 6c 64 21
```

If you go back to the ASCII table, you can compare each of these hexadecimal numbers with the ones you have there and build up the string `Hello, world!`. Because bytes objects only store integers, whenever you access an element of the sequence using a subscript (the index), what you retrieve is an integer:

```
>>> x = b"Hello, world!"
>>> x[0]
72
>>> x[1]
101
```

If you determine the integer represented the hexadecimal number 48 (the first pair from the hexadecimal representation of the *bytes* object), it's actually 72: $4 \times 16 + 8$.

2.2.2.4 Lists

Lists are a *mutable* sequence type that allow you to store arbitrary objects. Lists can be homogenous or heterogeneous regarding the objects they store. They can have zero or more elements and allow you to have repeated elements. Like strings and any other sequence type, you can create slices of lists in order to retrieve sublists with a subset of the elements. You can create lists in several ways. For example, by using square brackets:

```
>>> lis = []  # Creates an empty list
>>> lis
[]
>>> len(lis)
0
>>> lis = ["Stan", "Eric", "Kyle", "Kenny"]
>>> lis
['Stan', 'Eric', 'Kyle', 'Kenny']
>>> len(lis)
4
```

Assigning a variable just opening and closing square brackets creates an empty list. If you invoke the function **len** passing your variable as an argument, you will see that it returns 0. On the second example, I created a list with 4 elements of type *str*. The elements can be of any type, include *list*:

```
>>> lis1 = ["Stan", "Eric", "Kyle", "Kenny"]
>>> lis2 = [lis1, 1, 2, 3]
>>> lis2
[['Stan', 'Eric', 'Kyle', 'Kenny'], 1, 2, 3]
>>> type(lis2[0])
<class 'list'>
>>> type(lis2[1])
<class 'int'>
>>> lis2[1]
1
```

In this example, the second list has the first list as its first element and the remaining elements are integers.

Question: How do you retrieve `Kyle` from the list *lis2* by using subscript?

You can also create a list from an *iterable*. Remember what an *iterable* is? **Hint**: I explained it in Tuples data type section.

```
>>> lis = list("Hello, world!")
>>> lis
```

```
['H', 'e', 'l', 'l', 'o', ',', ' ', 'w', 'o', 'r', 'l',
'd', '!']
>>> lis = list((1, 2, 3))
>>> lis
[1, 2, 3]
```

In the first example, I'm creating a list from a string, which is an *iterable*. Each character from the string will become an element from the list. On the second example, I'm creating a list from a tuple with 3 elements. Again, each element from the tuple will become an element from the list.

There is another way of creating lists that I won't be introducing before *Control Flow*, which is called *lists comprehension*.

Let's now see a few operations that lists support. Well, for starters you can append elements to a list:

```
>>> lis = []
>>> lis.append("Stan")
>>> lis.append("Eric")
>>> lis
['Stan', 'Eric']
>>> lis.append("Kyle")
>>> lis
['Stan', 'Eric', 'Kyle']
>>> lis.append("Kenny")
>>> lis
['Stan', 'Eric', 'Kyle', 'Kenny']
```

You can also insert an element in the list before a certain index. The **insert** method receives two arguments: the *index* and an *object*, which is the element you want to insert. Remember what a method is? **Hint**: I gave a brief explanation in the Bytes data type section.

```
>>> lis.insert(1, "Randy")
>>> lis
['Stan', 'Randy', 'Eric', 'Kyle', 'Kenny']
```

In this example, I'm inserting the string `Randy` before the index 1. Because of that, the new element will have index 1. What if we try to insert before an index that goes beyond the size of the list?

```
>>> lis.insert(10, "Sharon")
>>> lis
['Stan', 'Randy', 'Eric', 'Kyle', 'Kenny', 'Sharon']
```

Not a problem, the new element is appended to the list.

Question: what happens if you try to insert an element before a negative index, like −2?

We can slice the list just the same way we sliced strings:

```
>>> lis
['Stan', 'Randy', 'Eric', 'Kyle', 'Kenny', 'Sharon']
>>> lis[2:]
['Eric', 'Kyle', 'Kenny', 'Sharon']
>>> lis[:4]
['Stan', 'Randy', 'Eric', 'Kyle']
>>> lis[::2]
['Stan', 'Eric', 'Kenny']
>>> lis[::-1]
['Sharon', 'Kenny', 'Kyle', 'Eric', 'Randy', 'Stan']
```

Here is how you can check what other operations are supported by lists:

```
>>> dir(list)
['__add__', '__class__', '__contains__', '__delattr__',
'__delitem__', '__dir__', '__doc__', '__eq__',
'__format__', '__ge__', '__getattribute__',
'__getitem__', '__gt__', '__hash__', '__iadd__',
'__imul__', '__init__', '__iter__', '__le__',
'__len__', '__lt__', '__mul__', '__ne__', '__new__',
'__reduce__', '__reduce_ex__', '__repr__',
'__reversed__', '__rmul__', '__setattr__',
'__setitem__', '__sizeof__', '__str__',
```

```
'__subclasshook__', 'append', 'clear', 'copy', 'count',
'extend', 'index', 'insert', 'pop', 'remove',
'reverse', 'sort']
>>>
```

If you enter the command **dir(list)** you will get a list of all the operations that you can do with objects with type list. For now, just focus on the methods that don't start with underscores.

If you want to know how to use a method, enter the command **help(list.<method-name>)**, such as **help(list.insert)**. This little documentation tells you that the method insert expects two parameters: an index and an object. It also tells you what the method will do: insert the object before the index. Press "q" to exit this documentation. Try exploring the documentation and do the same for the other types that you've learned so far.

2.2.2.5 ByteArrays

This is the last sequence type I will introduce. *ByteArray* is the mutable counterpart of Bytes: it supports the same operations and more, because it's mutable. I won't be spending much covering it. I will just provide a few examples on how to create a *bytearray* object and you can (and should) explore the rest yourself:

```
>>> b = bytearray()  # Creates an empty instance
>>> b
bytearray(b'')
>>> type(b)
<class 'bytearray'>
>>> b = bytearray(10)
>>> b
bytearray(b'\x00\x00\x00\x00\x00\x00\x00\x00\x00\x00')
```

The first example creates an empty *bytearray* object. The second one creates a *bytearray* object with length 10 and filled with zeros (the \x denotes hexadecimal number).

```
>>> bytearray.fromhex("48656c6c")
bytearray(b'Hell')
>>> b = bytearray(b"Hello, world!")
>>> b
bytearray(b'Hello, world!')
>>> b[0]
72
>>> b.hex()
'48656c6c6f2c20776f726c6421'
```

The method **fromhex** allows you to create a *bytearray* object from a string representing a hexadecimal number (without the \x prefix, though).

Honorable mention: *range*. The *range* type represents an immutable sequence of numbers, which is often used in `for` loops. I will explain this one better in *Control Flow* section.

2.2.2.6 Sequence Operators

In the table below you can find some common operations supported by sequence types, both mutable and immutable. Note that x represents an arbitrary object, s and t represent arbitrary sequence objects (string, tuple, bytes, etc) and *i, j, k* and *n* are integers.

Operation	Result
x in s	True if an element of s equals x, False otherwise
x not in s	True if no element of s equals x, False otherwise
s + t	s concatenated with t
s * n or n * s	s repeated *n* times
s[i]	Retrieves the element of s with position *i*, the counting starting on *0*

`s[i:j]`	Retrieves a slice of s from *i* to *j* (`s[j]` is not included)
`s[i:j:k]`	Retrieves a slice of s from *i* to *j* with step *k* (`s[j]` is not included)
`len(s)`	The number of elements in s (the length of s)
`min(s)`	The smallest element in s
`max(s)`	The largest element in s
`s.count(x)`	The number of occurrences of x in s

(*Sequence operators*)

A quick note regarding the multiplication operator (*****) with sequences. The resulting sequence doesn't have copies of the elements, but references to them instead:

```
>>> lis = [[1,2,3]]
>>> lis[0]
[1, 2, 3]
>>> lis2 = lis * 3
>>> lis2
[[1, 2, 3], [1, 2, 3], [1, 2, 3]]
```

We first create a list that contains one single element: a list with 3 integers. We then repeat that list 3 times and assign it to a new variable *lis2*. This new list doesn't have 3 copies of the element (the list with 3 integers), but 3 references to that element instead. This means that if you change any of these references, the others will have the change reflected:

```
>>> lis2[0].append(4)
>>> lis2
[[1, 2, 3, 4], [1, 2, 3, 4], [1, 2, 3, 4]]
>>> del lis2[1][2]
>>> lis2
[[1, 2, 4], [1, 2, 4], [1, 2, 4]]
```

The operator `del` is not available for immutable sequences for obvious reasons: they are immutable. `del lis2[1][2]` removes the third integer from the second list in *lis2*.

2.2.2.7 Notes on mutability and copying objects

If you remember what I've told you about variables, you know that they are a name bound to an object stored somewhere in memory. There is a built-in function in Python called **id**, which returns the identity of any object and is guaranteed to be unique. The CPython implementation (the one that we are using) returns the object's memory address.

```
>>> x = 1
>>> id(x)
4297854272
```

If you assign two names to the same object, you'll see that the **id** function returns the same value for both names:

```
>>> x = y = 1
>>> x
1
>>> y
1
>>> id(x)
4297854272
>>> id(y)
4297854272
```

This happens because `x` and `y` don't hold copies of the integer object with value 1: they both reference the same object stored in memory. Let's now see an example with a string:

```
>>> x = "Hello"
>>> id(x)
4304647536
>>> x = "world!"
>>> id(x)
4304647704
```

When you reassign a new value to x, the id changes because the name is being bound to a new string object stored in a different memory location. Some people say "Oh, a string is mutable because I can just reassign a new one to the variable". Well, my apologies to those folks, but what you are doing is actually creating a new string object and binding it to the name x, you are not changing the original object! Try to use the assignment operator on individual indexes, like this:

```
>>> x = "Hello"
>>> x[0] = "h"
Traceback (most recent call last):
  File "<stdin>", line 1, in <module>
TypeError: 'str' object does not support item
assignment
```

But lists are mutable and you can use the assignment operator on individual indexes or append elements. Which means that you are changing the same object that was initially bound to a name:

```
>>> x = [1, 2, 3]
>>> id(x)
4307611080
>>> x.append(4)
>>> x
[1, 2, 3, 4]
>>> id(x)
4307611080
```

Now that you understand why immutable objects are actually immutable, let me explain the difference between shallow and deep copies.

Lists are examples of compound types, because they can hold elements other than numbers or strings: you can have lists with lists or tuples as elements, or any other data types (that you may also define). When you make a shallow copy of a list, for example, what you get is a new compound object (a new list, in this case) with references to the objects found in the original list. If your list only holds immutable objects, this doesn't have much of an impact. But if that's not the case, then you need to be careful and, perhaps, consider deep copy instead.

Let's first take a look at a shallow copy in action:

```
>>> x = [["Hello", "world"], 1, 2, 3]
>>> y = x[:]
>>> y
[['Hello', 'world'], 1, 2, 3]
>>> id(x)
4307610056
>>> id(y)
4304652552
```

The name `y` is bound to a new list, as you can see by comparing **id(x)** with **id(y)**. But the original list bound to `x` contains another list as its first element, which means that the list bound to `y` will have a reference to that first element of the original list. So, if you change the first element of `x` (which is a list), it will affect `y` as well:

```
>>> x[0].append("Hi")
>>> y
[['Hello', 'world', 'Hi'], 1, 2, 3]
```

In order to avoid this situation is should use *deep copy*, instead. A deep copy will create a new compound object and also copies, recursively, of all the elements, instead of just placing references in the new compound object. By recursively I mean that if any of the elements contains other compound objects then the same deep copy mechanism will apply to them:

```
>>> import copy
>>> x = [["Hello", "world"], 1, 2, 3]
>>> y = copy.deepcopy(x)
>>> y
[['Hello', 'world'], 1, 2, 3]
>>> id(x)
4304652360
>>> id(y)
4307617800
>>> x[0].append("Hi")
>>> x
[['Hello', 'world', 'Hi'], 1, 2, 3]
>>> y
[['Hello', 'world'], 1, 2, 3]
```

Note that I had to *import* the module `copy`. You will learn everything you need about `import`, *modules* and *packages* further down the road. For now, just keep in mind the differences between shallow and deep copy, and the impact they can have on your code.

2.2.3 Sets

Sets represent an unordered collection of unique elements, which means that you cannot have duplicates. The elements in a set cannot be indexed, since sets are unordered. They **must also be _hashable_**, which means that you cannot have a list as an element of a set, because it's mutable and therefore not *hashable*.

But what does *hashable* mean? Recall the Hash Tables in Step 1: to calculate the index of a bucket in the array of values, the hash of the key is calculated, behind the scenes, using a hash function. Hashing is the process of transforming huge amounts of data into something much smaller, usually an integer, in an efficient way.

In Python, immutable objects are *hashable*, because their hash doesn't change during the object's lifetime. These objects also implement internally a **__hash__** method and their hash value is unique (like explained in Step 1). Both *sets* and *dictionaries* use the hash of their elements internally.

Sets are mutable and allow you to test elements membership (verify if an element is member of a set), remove duplicates from sequences and perform some mathematical operations like union and intersection. The immutable counterpart of *set* is called *frozenset*.

Let's play a bit with sets and I will also introduce you to the new operator **in**.

```
>>> s = {1}  # Creates a set with one element
>>> s
{1}
>>> s = {1, 2, 3}  # Creates a set with three elements
>>> s
{1, 2, 3}
>>> type(s)
<class 'set'>
>>> s = set()  # Creates an empty set
>>> len(s)
0
```

The built-in function **len** returns the number of members of the set. We can now add a few elements, including some duplicates and see how it goes:

```
>>> s.add("Randy")
>>> s
{'Randy'}
>>> s.add("Eric")
>>> s.add("Sharon")
>>> s
{'Eric', 'Randy', 'Sharon'}
>>> s.add("Eric")
```

```
>>> s
{'Eric', 'Randy', 'Sharon'}
```

As you can see, adding duplicates is gracefully handled: they are ignored. Let's now test membership using the **in** operator:

```
>>> "Kyle" in s
False
>>> "Kenny" in s
False
>>> "Eric" in s
True
```

The operator **in** tests if an element is **in** a set, if it's a member of the set. You can also use the operator **not in** to return the negation of **in**:

```
>>> "Eric" not in s
False
>>> "Kenny" not in s
True
```

The operators **in** and **not in** are supported by all the sequence and set types, as well as by dictionaries.

Question: how do the operators in and not in work with strings?

The *set* data type supports lots of operations. You can see it by entering the command **dir(set)** in the interactive shell. Let's just see a couple more and move on!

```
>>> s2 = set(["Kenny", "Kyle", "Eric", "Kenny",
⏎"Randy"])
>>> s2
{'Eric', 'Kenny', 'Randy', 'Kyle'}
```

We created a new set from a list that contained duplicates and they were gracefully ignored. Let's now perform some operations with our two sets:

```
>>> s.union(s2)
{'Sharon', 'Kenny', 'Eric', 'Randy', 'Kyle'}
```

The union **method** returns a new set that contains the elements of *s* and *s2*. Note that both *s* and *s2* remain unchanged. You can write it using a vertical bar (|) as well:

```
>>> s | s2
{'Sharon', 'Kenny', 'Eric', 'Randy', 'Kyle'}
```

The **intersection** method, on the other hand, returns a set with the common elements in both sets. This resulting set can be empty in case the two sets don't have any element in common.

```
>>> s.intersection(s2)
{'Eric', 'Randy'}
>>> s & s2  # Alternative way
{'Eric', 'Randy'}
```

Question 1: can you use slicing with sets?
Question 2: can you have a tuple as an element of a set?

2.2.4 Dictionaries

And this is the last built-in type that I will be introducing. Make sure you read thoroughly the section *Objects, Values and Types*[9] from the *Python Language Reference* as well as *Built-in Types*[6] from the *Python Standard Library*.

Dictionaries are a *mapping* type (they map keys to values) that represent a set of objects that can be indexed by pretty much any type of objects, as long as they are *hashable*. If you think of strings, tuples, lists and byte objects, their elements can only be indexed by integers. In dictionaries, you can use other objects to index the elements. Let's see dictionaries in practice:

```
>>> d = {}  # Creates an empty dictionary
>>> d
{}
>>> d = {"Eric": "Cartman", "Stan": "Marsh"}
>>> d
{'Eric': 'Cartman', 'Stan': 'Marsh'}
```

In the first example, we are creating an empty dictionary. In the second one, we are creating a dictionary with two values that are indexed by strings (the keys). The values are Cartman and Marsh. Let's see how can you retrieve these values:

```
>>> d["Eric"]
'Cartman'
>>> d["Stan"]
'Marsh'
```

Adding a new element to the dictionary is as easy as assigning a *value* to a non-existent *key*:

```
>>> d["Kyle"] = "Broflovski"
>>> d
{'Eric': 'Cartman', 'Stan': 'Marsh', 'Kyle':
'Broflovski'}
```

If you assign a new value to an existing key, then the old value will be replaced:

```
>>> d["Eric"] = "Cartmenez"
>>> d
{'Eric': 'Cartmenez', 'Stan': 'Marsh', 'Kyle':
'Broflovski'}
```

We're just getting started, but you'll soon see that dictionaries are perfect for organizing complex information temporarily. Here are some other possible ways of creating dictionaries:

```
>>> d = dict()  # Creates an empty dictionary
>>> d = dict({"Voodoo": 2000, "Resurrection": 1994,
↵"Liberation": 2006})
>>> d = dict(Eric="Cartman", Stan="Marsh")
>>> d
{'Eric': 'Cartman', 'Stan': 'Marsh'}
```

The first two ways of creating dictionaries are quite straightforward. The third one used something called *keyword arguments*. You will see (and use) *keyword arguments* quite often with functions, so I'll leave the explanation for the next section. Right now, all you need to know is that the keyword that you put on the left side of the assignment operator is subject to the same rules when you create a valid identifier (variable):

```
>>> d = dict(Eric Cartman=8, Stan="Marsh")
  File "<stdin>", line 1
    d = dict(Eric Cartman=8, Stan="Marsh")
                   ^
SyntaxError: invalid syntax
>>> d = dict(0Eric="Cartman", Stan="Marsh")
  File "<stdin>", line 1
    d = dict(0Eric="Cartman", Stan="Marsh")
             ^
SyntaxError: invalid syntax
```

The first example generates an error because `Eric Cartman` has a space character separating both words (you also can't create a variable that has a space character). The second example generates an error because the keyword `0Eric` starts with a digit (the same rules applies for variables, remember?)

> **Question**: what is the dictionary that results from `dict(Eric="Cartman", eric="Marsh")`?

You can also create dictionaries by providing a list of tuples as an argument to **dict**:

```
>>> d = dict([("Eric", 8), ("Randy", 40), ("Stan",
␣"Marsh")])
>>> d
{'Eric': 8, 'Randy': 40, 'Stan': 'Marsh'}
```

Note that each tuple must have 2 elements, where the first will be a key in the dictionary and the second will be the corresponding value. If you try to pass a tuple with more than 2 elements to the **dict** *constructor*, the interpreter will spit an error:

```
>>> d = dict([("Eric", "Cartman", 8), ("Randy", 40),
␣("Stan", "Marsh")])
Traceback (most recent call last):
  File "<stdin>", line 1, in <module>
ValueError: dictionary update sequence element #0 has
length 3; 2 is required
```

`#0` refers to the first element of the sequence you are providing as an argument.

Yet another way of building dictionaries is by using a **zip** object. A **zip** object is actually an *iterator* that is returned when you use the **zip** function. Like I explained briefly, an iterator

represents a stream of data and implements the method
__next__. Every time this method is invoked, the next element
from the stream is returned until the stream is exhausted. A
zip object is an iterator of *tuples*.

Let's see how **zip** works:

```
>>> z = zip(["a", "b", "c"], [1, 2, 3])
>>> z.__next__()
('a', 1)
>>> z.__next__()
('b', 2)
>>> z.__next__()
('c', 3)
>>> z.__next__()
Traceback (most recent call last):
  File "<stdin>", line 1, in <module>
StopIteration
```

In this example, I provided 2 arguments to **zip**, where each
argument is a sequence type (lists, for instance).

Recall now that you can pass any *iterable* object as an
argument to **list**. The method **__next__** of the *iterator*
associated to that *iterable* will be invoked until no more
elements are returned. This will build up a list with the
elements returned by the iterator.

```
>>> z = zip(["a", "b", "c"], [1, 2, 3])
>>> list(z)
[('a', 1), ('b', 2), ('c', 3)]
```

Both lists that I provided as arguments have the same length.
What happens if one of the lists is smaller than the other?

```
>>> z = zip(["a", "b", "c"], [1, 2, 3, 4])
>>> list(z)
[('a', 1), ('b', 2), ('c', 3)]
>>> z = zip(["a", "b", "c", "d"], [1, 2, 3])
>>> list(z)
[('a', 1), ('b', 2), ('c', 3)]
```

Then the resulting iterator will have as many elements as the length of the smallest sequence. And can you pass more than 2 sequences to zip? Of course you can. And can you imagine what would the resulting elements look like?

```
>>> z = zip(["a", "b", "c"], [1, 2, 3], ["Eric","Stan",
↵"Kyle"])
>>> list(z)
[('a', 1, 'Eric'), ('b', 2, 'Stan'), ('c', 3, 'Kyle')]
```

Nonetheless, when creating dictionaries using **zip** objects, we must only provide 2 sequences as arguments, or else the tuples won't have 2 elements (and you've seen previously that this is mandatory).

```
>>> d = dict(zip(["a", "b", "c"], [1, 2, 3]))
>>> d
{'b': 2, 'c': 3, 'a': 1}
```

You may have noticed that in the printed dictionary the elements didn't keep the same order as when you created the zip object. This is because dictionaries are unordered. It doesn't really matter, because you can retrieve the values given the correct key. But if by any chance you depend on the correct order of the keys, then you should consider using **OrderedDict** objects instead.

Question: what happens when you try to index a key that doesn't exist in a dictionary? For example d["abcd"]?

You can use the membership test operators **in** and **not in**, just like you use with sets. Note that, however, this will check whether the element you are testing is a *key* of the dictionary or not:

```
>>> d = {"Eric": 8, "Stan": 9, "Randy": 40}
>>> 8 in d
False
>>> "Eric" in d
True
```

There are three methods that return *view objects*: **dict.keys()**, **dict.values()** and **dict.items()**. *View objects* provide a dynamic view on the dictionary's entries. So, whenever the dictionary changes, those objects also change. Let's see how it works:

```
>>> d = {"Eric": 8, "Stan": 9, "Randy": 40}
>>> keys = d.keys()  # This is a view object
>>> keys
dict_keys(['Eric', 'Randy', 'Stan'])
>>> list(keys)
['Eric', 'Randy', 'Stan']
```

In this example, the variable `keys` was assigned the *view object* returned when invoking the method **keys()** on the dictionary. The variable `keys` provides a dynamic view over the keys in the dictionary. What will happen to that variable if the keys of the dictionary change? Let's delete one of the keys (and the corresponding value) and check the contents of the variable:

```
>>> del d["Eric"]
>>> d
{'Randy': 40, 'Stan': 9}
>>> list(keys)
['Randy', 'Stan']
```

The first operation `del` will remove `d["Eric"]` from the dictionary.

And as you can see, I didn't have to reassign **d.keys()** to the `keys` variable again, because the *view* was updated. Try doing the same with **d.values()**!

Let's see now what happens with **d.items()**:

```
>>> d = {"Eric": 8, "Stan": 9, "Randy": 40}
>>> d
{'Eric': 8, 'Randy': 40, 'Stan': 9}
>>> items = d.items()
>>> items
dict_items([('Eric', 8), ('Randy', 40), ('Stan', 9)])
>>> list(items)
[('Eric', 8), ('Randy', 40), ('Stan', 9)]
```

The *view object* returned by **d.items()** provides a dynamic view over tuples that represent key/value pairs from the dictionary. Again, if something changes in the dictionary, this *view object* will reflect the changes:

```
>>> d["Stan"] = 10
>>> list(items)
[('Eric', 8), ('Randy', 40), ('Stan', 10)]
>>> del d["Randy"]
>>> list(items)
[('Eric', 8), ('Stan', 10)]
```

As expected, right? These 3 *view objects* are very often used in `for` loops, when you need to iterate over a dictionary (either its keys, its values or its items).

We're done for now regarding *data types*. Other data types will be introduced as needed, but you can do pretty much anything with these. The others that I didn't introduce now are either more performant or more convenient, hence suitable for more advanced and specific use cases.

Nonetheless, there is an honorable mention: the **None** type. There is one single object with this type and the object is called None. This object is used to express the absence of value, for example in situations where no value is returned. This may sound a bit confusing, but think of a function or a method. They may or may not return a value. So far, all the functions and methods that we used returned something, but this is not always the case. For example, the method **sort()** from list objects doesn't return anything explicitly, so by default the object None is returned to express that nothing is being returned:

```
>>> lis = [3, 2, 4, 7, 6]
>>> value = lis.sort()
>>> value is None
True
>>> lis
[2, 3, 4, 6, 7]
```

The truth value of None is False.

2.2.5 A little recap

Something that can be a bit confusing for whoever is starting with programming (or even with Python) is to visually distinguish between a list, a tuple, a set or a dictionary. Too many curly braces, square brackets and parentheses can make your life harder! As such, here's a little cheat table with the different forms that each of those can assume:

Form	Description
x = [1, 2, 3]	**List** with three integers
x = (1, 2, 3)	**Tuple** with three integers
x = 1, 2, 3	**Tuple** with three integers
x = [(1, 2), (3, 4)]	**List** with two **Tuples**
x = ([1, 2], [3, 4])	**Tuple** with two **Lists**
x = {1, 2, 3}	**Set** with three integers
x = {(1, 2), (3, 4)}	**Set** with two tuples (note that the elements of a set must be *hashable*)
x = {"a": 1, "b": 2}	**Dictionary** with two keys (strings) and their corresponding values (integers)

Elements separated by commas inside square brackets (**[ ]**) are **lists**. Elements separated by commas without any enclosing symbols or enclosed by parentheses are **tuples**. Elements separated by commas enclosed by curly braces (**{ }**) are **sets**. Elements with the form `key:value` separated by commas inside curly braces are **dictionaries**.

2.3 More Operators

2.3.1 Boolean Operators

Boolean operations return a truth value depending on the truth value of each of the operands. They are similar to the bitwise operations introduced in Step 1 in the section regarding Binary Numbers. `True` and `False` can be thought of as abstractions to the integers 1 and 0, respectively. `x` and `y` are arbitrary expressions that hold a truth value, either `True` or `False`.

Operation	Result
x and y	True if both x and y are True, False otherwise
x or y	False if both x and y are False, True otherwise
not x	True if x is False, False otherwise

(*Boolean Operators*)

Both **or** and **and** are *short-circuit* operators. This means that when performing a *boolean* **and**, y is only evaluated if x is True. On the other hand, when performing a *boolean* **or**, y is only evaluated if x is False.

2.3.2 Comparison Operators

Comparison operations return a *boolean* that represents the truth value of the expression. Note that the truth value depends on the type of the objects you are trying to compare.

Operation	Result
x < y	True if x is strictly less than y, False otherwise
x <= y	True if x is less than or equal to y, False otherwise
x > y	True if x is strictly greater than y, False otherwise
x >= y	True if x is greater than or equal to y, False otherwise
x == y	True if x equals y, False otherwise
x != y	True if x is different from y, False otherwise
x is y	True if x and y are the same object, False otherwise

| x is not y | True if x and y are different object, False otherwise |

(Comparison Operators)

The behavior of these operations depends on the type of objects. It's worth mentioning that the operators <, <=, > and >= cannot be applied to objects of different types.

When comparing integers or real numbers, the result is quite obvious, but for the complete beginner this may not be the case when comparing strings or lists. Let's see why:

```
>>> "zorro" < "aaaaaaaa"
False
>>> "zorro" < "zzaaaaaa"
True
```

Even though the string aaaaaaaa is longer than the string zorro, it's actually *lexicographically* smaller. When comparing two words lexicographically, the *alphabetical order* of each letter matters. In the first comparison, the letter z is lexicographically greater than the letter a (it comes later in the alphabet), so we don't need to compare any further. In the second comparison, the letter z in zorro has the same alphabetic order as the first z in zzaaaaaa, so we compare the second letter of each word. The second letter of zorro, o, has a smaller alphabetic order than the second z of zzaaaaaa, so we can stop the comparison because the second word is lexicographically greater.

Another thing worth mentioning is that when you are comparing two lists x and y using the operators <, <=, > and >=, you need to make sure that for every index $i < n$, x[i] and y[i] have the same type. In this case, i is an integer and n is an integer that represents the length of the smallest list.

```
>>> [1, 2] < [1, "a"]
Traceback (most recent call last):
  File "<stdin>", line 1, in <module>
TypeError: unorderable types: int() < str()
```

In this situation, the interpreter complains because on the second position the two lists have elements of different type: an integer and a string.

```
>>> [1, 2, 3, "a"] > [1, 2, 3]
True
```

Why did this work? Well, even though $1 > 1$ is `False`, the thing is that the smallest list is a subsequence of the longest one.

Question: what is the result of `[2, 7, 3, "a"] > [1, 6, 4]`?

2.3.3 Operators Precedence

Different types of Operations have different priorities. The priority of an operation determines whether the interpreter will perform such operation before or after another operation in the same expression. For example, arithmetic multiplication has higher precedence than arithmetic addition:

```
>>> 1 + 2 * 3
7
```

If you wanted the result to be 9, then you should use parentheses:

```
>>> (1 + 2) * 3
9
```

The table below contains all the operators ordered by priority and precedence, as described in the section *Operator Precedence*[11] from *Python Language Reference*. Operators with highest priority are at the bottom of the table and every row has the same level of priority.

Operator	Description
lambda	Lambda expression
if - else	Conditional expression
x or y	Boolean OR
x and y	Boolean AND
not x	Boolean NOT
in, not in, is, is not, <, <=, >, >=, ==, !=	Comparisons, membership test and identity test
x | y	Bitwise OR
x^y	Bitwise XOR
x & y	Bitwise AND
x << n ,x >> n	Bitwise shift (left and right)
+, -	addition and subtraction
*, @, /, //, %	Multiplication, matrix multiplication, division, integer division and remainder
+x, -x, ~x	Positive, negative and bitwise NOT
x**y	Exponentiation (x to the power y)
await x	Await expression
x[index], x[index:index], x(arguments...), x.attribute	Subscription, slicing, call and attribute reference

| `(expressions...)`,
`[expressions...]`,
`{key:value...}`, `{expressions...}` | Bind or tuple display, list display,
dictionary display and set display |

(*Operators Precedence*)

2.4 Control Flow and Functions

When writing software, even if it's a small application, you will be doing more than just assigning values to variables or performing basic operations. Unless, of course, you intend to use Python just as a calculator, which is perfectly fine and not that unusual. But even when you want to use certain mathematical models, you will probably have to use control flow constructs, in order to make your life easier.

Typical control flow constructs are **if**, **while** and **for**. They are also called compound statements, because they contain one or more statements. Python uses indentation to determine whether a statement belongs to a compound statement or not, but this is not necessary in some cases. Other compound statements are **try** (which we will explore in the section *Handling Errors and Exceptions*) and **with** (we'll explore in the next section, *Handling Files*). **Functions** and **Class definitions** are also considered compound statements. Classes will be introduced in *Object Oriented Programming* section.

2.4.1 `if` Statement

The `if` statement is probably one of the most widely known control flow constructs and it is used for conditional execution. It's made of a mandatory `if` block, zero or more `elif` blocks and an optional `else` block.

In Python, a group of statements is also called a *suite*. All the statements that belong to the same *suite* must be at the same level of indentation, and their level of indentation must be greater than the indentation level of header of the block (the header is either `if`, `elif` or `else`). Statements are separated by `NEWLINE` characters, meaning that each statement must be placed on a separate line.

> **Note**: if you are a beginner to Python but come from other programming languages like Java, PHP or C, you may find this confusing. In those languages (and many other), each statement must terminate with a semicolon and you group them using curly braces { }. This is not the case in Python: proper indentation is your curly braces. Statements can still have a semicolon at the end, even though this is not mandatory, unless you have more than one on the same line. As a good practice and to promote code readability, you should have one statement per line.

The expressions hold a truth value. The `if` statement selects one of the *suites* to be executed by evaluating the expressions, until the first being `True` is found. If none of the expressions is `True`, then the *suite* from the `else` block is executed, if the `else` block is present.

```
If <expression>:
    statement
    statement
    (...)
elif <expression>:
    statement
    statement
    (...)
else:
    statement
    statement
    (...)
```

Let's stop using the interpreter in interactive mode and start writing Python code in a file instead.

Create a file wherever you want. I called my file *controlflow.py*, so feel free to do the same.

> **Note**: A Python file is a normal text file, but with an extension *py*. You can create it and write your Python code with whatever Text Editor you prefer, even Notepad if

you are in Windows. I prefer to work on the command-line. My editor of choice in Mac OS X and Linux is Vim. If you are in Mac or Linux, just type `vim controlflow.py` and hit *Enter*. There is also the *Nano* editor, which is simpler but also less powerful than *Vim*. If you want to learn the basics of Vim, I strongly recommend playing the online game *Vim Adventures*[11].

Copy and paste the code in the box below to the file, save it and go back to the command-line if you were not there already.

Now in the directory where your file is, type `python controlflow.py` and hit *Enter*. If you want to navigate through directories, use the command `cd` (which stands for *change directory*). `cd directory_name` enters a directory called `directory _name`, as long as such directory exists in the directory where you execute the `cd` from. If afterwards you type `cd ..` then you will go back to where you were.

```python
age = int(input("Enter your age: "))
if age >= 30:
    print("You are 30 or above.")
elif 20 <= age < 30:
    print("You are in your twenties.")
else:
    print("You are below 20.")
```

(file controlflow.py)

Without much effort, you probably can understand most of this script, if not all. The only thing that maybe confused you a bit was the sequence **int(input("..."))** in the first line.

The built-in function **input** reads a string from the *standard input*, which in this case is your keyboard. I am passing the string `Enter your age:` as an argument to the function. This is called the *prompt string*, but it's not necessary. You may remember the built-in function **int()** from the table with *Numeric Operations*: it converts the argument into an integer. In this case, we are converting whatever string with digits you enter into an integer. Note that the **int()** function fails if the string contains characters that are not digits.

Let's give it a try:

```
→ ~/StartCareerPython python controlflow.py
Enter your age: 34
You are 30 or above.
```

Make some experiments yourself! Try to remove the `elif` block and see how this code behaves. Then remove the `else` block instead and see how it behaves.

Note that the `elif` could have been written the following way:

```
elif age >= 20 and age < 30:
```

Now that we have knowledge of this powerful construct, let's build something a bit more complex. I will be introducing new functions and methods along the way, so be sure to use the help in the interactive shell whenever you need.

The challenge is to write a small program that receives a string with words separated by commas and creates a list where each element is a word from that string. If the length of the list is an even number, we sort the list in **ascending** alphabetical order, or else we will sort in **descending** alphabetical order. The list should be printed at the end. Also, assume that the input is always correct, meaning that it will always be a string with words separated by commas.

Sample input 1: dog,tree,car,red,grape,water,blue,sky
Sample output 1: ['blue', 'car', 'dog', 'grape', 'red', 'sky', 'tree', 'water']

Sample input 2: dog,tree,car,red,grape,water,blue
Sample output 2: ['water', 'tree', 'red', 'grape', 'dog', 'car', 'blue']

105

```
1 string = input("Enter your string: ")
2 string_list = string.split(",")
3 if len(string_list) % 2 == 0:
4     print(sorted(string_list))
5 else:
6     print(sorted(string_list, reverse=True))
```

Let's dissect the code to make sure you understand what's going on here.

- On line 1, we are reading a string from the *standard input* and assigning it to the variable `string`. Nothing special here.

- On line 2 I'm introducing the method **split** that operates on string objects. Run the interpreter in interactive mode and enter the command **help(str.split)**. The method **split** accepts two optional *parameters*, one of them being *sep*. If *sep* is provided when you invoke split, then the method will return a list with the words in the string, using *sep* as a delimiter. In our little script, I used the comma character as a delimiter. If you don't provide *sep*, then the method will use any whitespace character as a delimiter and empty strings will be removed from the result.

- Confused with the operation in line 3? I'm just performing a parity check. The operator `%` returns the remainder of the division between the length of the list and 2. If the remainder is 0, it means that the number is even. This could actually have been achieved with a much shorter version: `if not len(string_list) % 2`. There are certain values that in Python evaluate to `False`, including 0 of any numeric type. This means that `not 0` holds the same truth value as `not False`, which is `True`. Make sure to check the section *Truth Value Testing*[12] from *Python Standard Library*.

- The only thing worth mentioning in lines 4, 5 and 6 is the usage of **sorted()**. The built-in function **sorted()** returns a list with the elements of an iterable sorted in ascending order. Note that all the elements of the *iterable* must have the same type. If the *iterable* is a string, then this is not a problem, but if the *iterable* is a string or a tuple, you must make sure that this condition is verified. If you provide the *key*, then it will be used to customize the order, or else the elements will be compared directly. If the keyword argument *reverse* is provided and is True, then the list will be sorted in descending order. If it's not provided, then it defaults to False. Let's see an example of providing a *key* for the sort order:

```
>>> sorted("Pedro")
['P', 'd', 'e', 'o', 'r']
>>> sorted("Pedro", key=str.lower)
['d', 'e', 'o', 'P', 'r']
```

The second time I invoke **sorted**, I specify the method **lower** as key. The method **lower** is applied to string objects and returns a copy of the string in lowercase.

```
>>> string = "PedRo"
>>> string.lower()
'pedro'
```

So how is the *key* used by **sorted**? Well, sorted works by comparing pairs of elements in the *iterable*. When *key* is provided, it will be applied to each of the elements that are being compared before making the comparison. It **DOES NOT** change the elements. The first time I applied **sorted**, the letter P came in first place because capital letters have lower alphabetic order. The second time **sorted** was applied, the method **lower** was applied to P, so it was treated as being lowercase.

2.4.1.1 Some notes on logic

As a beginner, it's perfectly normal for you to write conditional expressions in their full extension, because they explicitly translate your intentions. For example, when you have a number x and you want to do something in case x is even, you would naturally write it as follows:

```
if x % 2 == 0:
    print("It's even")
```

This is perfectly correct and does what you want: if x is even, then print It's even. Which means that you want to print the string in case the expression in the if statement evaluates to True.

There is, although, another way to write this and still have a coherent truth value for that expression. Let's start by removing the == 0 from the expression:

```
if x % 2:
    print("It's even")
```

The expression evaluates to 0, which holds a truth value of False. So the behavior would be the opposite of what we wanted. In order to turn that into a True for even numbers, we must negate the False:

```
if not x % 2:
    print("It's even")
```

Now, if the number is even, the expression will be if not 0 or if not False, which is the same as if True. What

108

if `x` is odd? Then `x % 2` will be different than `0`, which will hold the truth value `True`. But because we are negating it, the end result will be `if not True`, which is the same as `if False`. So the string won't be printed.

At the end of the day, what we want is to **do something if the conditional expression evaluates to `True` for every even number**.

The conditional expressions are subject to logical operations, and many times they can be simplified, as long as they hold the same expressiveness and coherence. The following table gives you some hints on logical operations, which hopefully will help you fully understand and write better conditional expressions:

Expression	Equivalent
not (not **A**)	**A**
not (**A** or **B**)	(not **A**) and (not **B**)
A or **B**	**B** or **A**
not (**A** and **B**)	(not **A**) or (not **B**)
A and **B**	**B** and **A**

(Logical equivalences)

A and **B** are expressions whose evaluation holds a truth value (for example, `x % 2` or `x % 2 == 0`).

2.4.1.2 Some notes on indentation
Python forces you to write code properly indented. In other languages, as long as you have curly braces properly placed, you'll get the result you want even if your code is ugly and completely unreadable. In Python, you can very easily determine if a statement makes part of a certain suite or not just by looking at the indentation level. This applies to pretty

much everything, such as `if` statements, `for` and `while` loops, function and class definitions, etc.

If you already have programming experience, you can grasp this concept immediately, but still see it as an annoyance. For complete beginners, though, this can be a bit harder. Let me show you some examples of indentation levels (**note**: experienced programmers may want to skip this part):

```
if x % 2 == 0:
    print("It's even")
    print("Still part of the if")
print("Not part of the if")
```

If `x` is an even number, then all the three **print** functions are executed. If `x` is not an even number, only the last **print** is executed. Let's see another example:

```
if not x % 2:
    print("It's even")
    if x < 100:
        print("It's smaller than 100")
    else:
        print("It's greater than 100)
    print("Done")
else:
    print("It's not even")
```

What happens when `x` is 44? It's both even and smaller than 100, so here's what's executed (in bold):

```
if not x % 2:
    print("It's even")
    if x < 100:
        print("It's smaller than 100")
    else:
        print("It's greater than 100)
    print("Done")
else:
    print("It's not even")
```

What if x is 202?

```
if not x % 2:
    print("It's even")
    if x < 100:
        print("It's smaller than 100")
    else:
        print("It's greater than 100)
    print("Done")
else:
    print("It's not even")
```

And 301?

```
if not x % 2:
    print("It's even")
    if x < 100:
        print("It's smaller than 100")
    else:
        print("It's greater than 100)
    print("Done")
else:
    print("It's not even")
```

2.4.2 `for` Statement

The `for` statement allows you to iterate over the elements of an *iterable*, such as sequence types (string, tuple or list). Let's start with a very simple example (using the interactive shell) before going to the formal definition:

```
>>> string = "Test"
>>> for c in string:
...     print(c)
...
T
e
s
t
```

An *iterator* will be created for `string`. For each item returned by the iterator, that item will be assigned to the variable `c` and the function **print** will be executed.

> **Note**: the 3 dots (...) are a secondary prompt in the interactive shell (the primary prompt is >>>). They indicate continuation lines, which are needed when you enter a multi-line statement.

The generic form of the `for` statement is as follows:

```
for target_list in expression_list:
    suite
else:
    suite
```

The `expression_list` yields an *iterable* object, from which an iterator is created and is executed only once. Like I mentioned before, for each item returned by the iterator, the item is assigned to `target_list` and the first *suite* is executed. When there are no more items to be returned by the iterator, the suite in the `else` clause, if present, is executed.

2.4.2.1 Variables revisited

So far, we've only assigned values to one variable at a time, but Python supports multi-assignment, which is represented by the `target_list` in the `for` statement.

```
>>> a, b = 0, "word"
>>> a
0
>>> b
'word'
```

We can also unpack items from a sequence type to variables, but the number of variables being assigned must match the number of items being unpacked:

```
>>> name, age = ("Eric", 8)
>>> name
'Eric'
>>> age
8
>>> name, age = ["Eric", 8]
>>> name
'Eric'
>>> age
8
>>> name, age, country = ["Eric", 8]
Traceback (most recent call last):
 File "<stdin>", line 1, in <module>
ValueError: not enough values to unpack (expected 3,
got 2)
```

Multi-assignment is quite useful (and normal) in `for` statements:

```
>>> students_grades = [("John", "A"), ("Sarah", "B"),
⌐ ("Bob", "A-")]
>>> for student, grade in students_grades:
...     print("Name: {}, Grade: {}".format(student,
⌐grade))
...
Name: John, Grade: A
Name: Sarah, Grade: B
Name: Bob, Grade: A-
```

The method **format** returns a formatted version of the string, using its arguments to replace the curly braces in the string. There is a bit more to this method, which we'll explore later.

2.4.2.2 Types revisited: `range` and `iterator`

With `for` statements it makes sense to introduce two other data types: *range* and *iterator*.

113

Range

The *range* type represents an immutable sequence of numbers and is useful when you want to loop in a `for` loop for a specific number of times. Because this is a sequence type, it is also subject to normal sequence operations, such as *slicing* and *indexing*.

```
>>> for i in range(5):
...     print(i)
...
0
1
2
3
4
>>> for i in range(2, 7):
...     print(i)
...
2
3
4
5
6
>>> list(range(2, 7))
[2, 3, 4, 5, 6]
>>> list(range(0, 10, 2))
[0, 2, 4, 6, 8]
```

If you just provide one argument, it will be interpreted as the *stop* (or the length of the sequence). When providing two arguments, they will be interpreted as *start* and *stop*. If you omit the *step* by providing just two arguments, the *step* will default to 1, just like when you are *slicing*. If a third argument is provided, it will be the *step*. Just like when slicing, the *step* can be negative.

Using a *range* object to loop is better than using a *list* or *tuple* with integers, because independently of the size of the sequence, the same (small) amount of memory will always be used. In fact, only the *start*, *stop* and *step* are stored, all the subsequent values are calculated as needed.

If you want to iterate over the items of a sequence and their indices, however, it's more convenient to use the built-in function **enumerate**, which takes an *iterable* as an argument (and an optional *start* index).

```
>>> names = ["John", "Mary", "Bob", "Sarah"]
>>> for i, name in enumerate(names):
...     print(i, name)
...
0 John
1 Mary
2 Bob
3 Sarah
```

The built-in function **enumerate()** returns an object from which an iterator is created. On every iteration, this object returns a tuple that contains a count (from *start*, which is assume to be zero if not provided) and the current item of the sequence.

Question: given the previous example, can you provide another way of iterating over the names in the sequence and their indices without using enumerate?

Iterator

You already know a bit about this. *Iterables* are container objects that are capable of returning their elements one at a time. They can be *lists*, *strings*, *tuples*, *dictionaries*, etc. They return their elements one at a time via an **iterator**.

The *iterable* objects implement a method called **__iter__** that returns an *iterator* for that object. An *iterator* is an object that represents a stream of data.

Whenever an *iterable* object is passed to a `for` loop or to an `in` statement, its **__iter__** method is invoked and the iterator is returned. The iterator, on the other hand, implements two methods, in order to be compliant with the *iterator protocol*: **__iter__** and **__next__**. The method **__iter__** allows the iterator to return itself and the method **__next__** returns the next item from the container (from the *iterable*). As soon as there are no more items to be returned, the method **__next__** will raise an *exception* StopIteration and will continue to do so for every subsequent call to the method.

You've already seen this with **zip** objects. Let's see this in action for a list of strings. A list of strings is an *iterable* object, which means that it contains a method **__iter__**.

```
>>> l = ["red", "green", "blue", "yellow", "white",
⌐ "black", "orange"]
>>> iterator = l.__iter__()
>>> iterator
<list_iterator object at 0x108f231d0>
>>> type(iterator)
<class 'list_iterator'>
```

The variable iterator yields the *iterator* for the list. Which means that it has, amongst others, two methods: **__iter__** and **__next__**. We're interested in using **__next__** to retrieve the elements from the list one at a time. As you will probably guess, as soon as we retrieve the string orange, the method **__next__** will start raising StopIteration *exceptions*.

```
>>> iterator.__next__()
'red'
>>> iterator.__next__()
'green'
>>> iterator.__next__()
'blue'
>>> iterator.__next__()
'yellow'
>>> iterator.__next__()
'white'
>>> iterator.__next__()
'black'
>>> iterator.__next__()
'orange'
>>> iterator.__next__()
Traceback (most recent call last):
```

```
  File "<stdin>", line 1, in <module>
StopIteration
>>> iterator.__next__()
Traceback (most recent call last):
  File "<stdin>", line 1, in <module>
StopIteration
```

Whenever you pass an *iterable* object to a `for` loop or to an `in` statement, a fresh new *iterator* object is returned, in order for you to be able to retrieve elements one by one starting from the beginning. More about Iterators can be found in the section *Iterator Types*[13] from *Python Standard Library*.

2.4.2.3 Nested `for` loops

You can also have nested `for` loops, especially when you have containers inside containers.

```
for container in main_container:
    for element in container:
        <do something 1>
    <do something 2>
```

The inner `for` loop is executed as many times as the number of containers inside `main_container`. For every container inside `main_container`, the *<do something 1>* suite is executed as many times as the number of elements inside that container. The *<do something 2>* suite is executed every time the inner `for` loop ends.

Let's see this in action, with a list that contains lists of strings:

```
>>> months = [
... ["Jan", "Feb", "Mar"],
... ["Apr", "May", "Jun"],
... ["Jul", "Aug", "Sep"],
... ["Oct", "Nov", "Dec"]]
```

The list could have been written in a flat way, but like this is easier for you to visualize it. Say we want to print the months of each quarter separated by the string `End of Quarter n`. Here's one way of achieving it with nested `for` loops:

```
>>> for q, quarter in enumerate(months, 1):
...     for month in quarter:
...         print(month, end=" ")
...     print("\nEnd of quarter {}".format(q))
...
Jan Feb Mar
End of quarter 1
Apr May Jun
End of quarter 2
Jul Aug Sep
End of quarter 3
Oct Nov Dec
End of quarter 4
```

Try to digest the code for a bit so that you can understand it on your own and pay close attention to the indentation of the code. Remember what does the built-in **enumerate** function return? What are the values of `quarter` in the outer `for` loop? And why did I provide a second argument to the **print** function? What about the values of `month` in the inner `for` loop?

If you still weren't able to fully understand nested `for` loops, don't despair, for the explanation is on its way!

The outer `for` loop is executed 4 times, one for each list inside `months`. The variable `q` holds the count returned by **enumerate** (starting at 1) and the variable `quarter` holds the current list from `months`, also returned by **enumerate**.

The inner `for` loop is executed for each quarter as many times as the number of elements that the list held by `quarter` contains (3, in this example). The variable `month` in the inner `for` loop holds each element from the current list stored in `quarter`.

The second argument, `end`, in the first **print()** determines the character used to terminate the string that you are printing. If not specified, it will default to `\n`, which is a *newline* character, but in this case I wanted to have the months separated by one space character.

Of course, this is a silly example, but my point is just to illustrate nested `for` loops. The same result can be achieved with much smaller code:

```
>>> for q, quarter in enumerate(months, 1):
...     print(" ".join(quarter))
...     print("End of quarter {}".format(q))
...
```

The method **join** does the opposite of what **split** does: it takes a list of strings and returns a string with the elements concatenated using the string as a separator. In this case, the separator string is a space character. If you wanted to use a comma to separate the months instead, you would do it like this:

```
",".join(quarter)
```

Here's an example of join in action:

```
>>> ",".join(["Jan", "Feb", "Mar"])
'Jan,Feb,Mar'
```

The code could be even smaller! But remember, as a good practice, you should aim for readability. One liners with lots of code are far from being readable and make it harder to debug and understand, but it can be fun and it's definitely a good way to practice your mental agility:

```
>>> print("\n".join(["{}\nEnd of quarter {}".format("
↵".join(quarter), q) for q, quarter in
↵enumerate(months,1)]))

Jan Feb Mar
End of quarter 1
Apr May Jun
End of quarter 2
Jul Aug Sep
End of quarter 3
Oct Nov Dec
End of quarter 4
```

I leave it as an exercise for you to try to understand what I wrote. Like I said, one liners are great to practice mental agility, but avoid them as much as you can. Your colleagues (and yourself) will appreciate it.

2.4.2.4 Lists revisited: list comprehension

Now that you have an understanding of how `for` loops work, it's time to introduce another way of creating lists: using *list comprehensions*. Let's first create a list using the "regular" way. Imagine that you have a list of strings and now you want to create a second list containing strings from the first one, but only strings with length greater than 5 characters.

```
>>> lis = ["New York", "California", "Utah", "Florida",
↵"Illinois", "Texas"]
```

`Texas` and `Utah` will be excluded from the second list. The "regular" way of building the second list is to iterate over the first list with a `for` loop and append the strings that match the criteria to an empty list previously created.

```
>>> lis2 = []
>>> for c in lis:
...     if len(c) > 5:
...         lis2.append(c)
```

```
...
>>> print(lis2)
['New York', 'California', 'Florida', 'Illinois']
```

Nothing special here: we are iterating over the elements of lis; if the length of the current element (stored in the variable c) is greater than 5, then we append that element to lis2, the empty list previously created. At the end, we print the list just to confirm everything is fine.

However, if we want to use *list comprehensions*, the solution will be slightly different:

```
>>> lis2 = [c for c in lis if len(c) > 5]
>>> print(lis2)
['New York', 'California', 'Florida', 'Illinois']
```

Yep, it's just that first line. Can you understand what's happening there? Most likely you can, but in case you are still a bit confused, let's play with some more examples. What if you want the elements of the new list to be in lowercase?

```
>>> lis2 = [c.lower() for c in lis if len(c) > 5]
>>> print(lis2)
['new york', 'california', 'florida', 'illinois']
```

Imagine that now we only want the elements whose last character is the letter a (**hint**: use a negative index).

```
>>> lis2 = [c for c in lis if c[-1] == "a"]
>>> print(lis2)
['California', 'Florida']
```

What if you want only the elements whose last character is the letter a **or** have a length greater than 5?

```
>>> lis2 = [c for c in lis if c[-1] == "a" or len(c) >
⌙5]
>>> print(lis2)
['New York', 'California', 'Florida', 'Illinois']
```

2.4.2.5 Dictionaries revisited: dict comprehension

Dictionary comprehensions work in a similar way, but the difference is that you must extract both the key and the value from whatever expression you use in the `for` loop.

Let's see a simple example of a dictionary whose keys are all the even numbers between 0 and 12 (exclusive) and the values are the square of the key:

```
>>> d = {}
>>> for x in range(0, 12):
...     if x % 2 == 0:
...         d[x] = x**2
...
>>> d
{0: 0, 2: 4, 4: 16, 6: 36, 8: 64, 10: 100}
```

And now with *dict comprehension*:

```
>>> {x:x**2 for x in range(0, 12) if x % 2 == 0}
{0: 0, 2: 4, 4: 16, 6: 36, 8: 64, 10: 100}
```

Both the *key* and the *value* can be built just using the variable x. Of course, we can be more clever and use the step to avoid the `if` statement (which is there to ensure that x is an even number).

```
>>> {x:x**2 for x in range(0, 12, 2)}
{0: 0, 2: 4, 4: 16, 6: 36, 8: 64, 10: 100}
```

Let's see yet another example, where the key and the value are fetched from different variables:

```
>>> names = ["Eric", "Stan", "Kyle", "Kenny"]
>>> {name:index for index,name in enumerate(names)}
{'Kenny': 3, 'Kyle': 2, 'Stan': 1, 'Eric': 0}
```

Now, the most attentive reader might be thinking "Why the hell did he use a *dict comprehension* instead of passing the **enumerate** directly to **dict**?". Yes, you are absolutely right!

```
>>> dict(enumerate(names))
{0: 'Eric', 1: 'Stan', 2: 'Kyle', 3: 'Kenny'}
```

Challenge: Remember the list containing lists with months? Now the idea is for you to build a dictionary (using *dict comprehension*) where each key is a string with the form `Quarter` n and the corresponding value is a list with the months of that quarter. Here's what your dictionary should look like:

```
{'Quarter 4': ['Oct', 'Nov', 'Dec'], 'Quarter 2':
['Apr', 'May', 'Jun'], 'Quarter 1': ['Jan', 'Feb',
'Mar'], 'Quarter 3': ['Jul', 'Aug', 'Sep']}
```

Hint: use the string method **format** and the built-in **enumerate**.

2.4.2.6 A note on comprehensions

Both *list* and *dict comprehensions* may seem a bit confusing at the beginning, but as soon as it makes a click in your brain, you will feel like a Jedi! Let me be like Yoda while you give me a piggyback ride through the swamps.

The general form of building a list using a `for` loop is:

1. You define an empty list.
2. You define the header of the `for` loop.
3. You append the element to the list in the body of the `for` loop, perhaps after doing something to the element.

So it looks like this:

```
lis = []
for item in some_iterable:
    x = do_something(item)
    lis.append(x)
```

The reason why I added the do_something line is because if you are building a list where each element is an element from the *iterable*, then you can just use **list(some_iterable)** instead.

Turning the traditional for loop form into a list comprehension is as easy as follows:

```
lis = [do_something(item) for item in some_iterable]
```

You don't even need the **append** part, because that is implicit in the *comprehension*.

What about *dict comprehensions*? Well, let's first take a look at the traditional way of building up a dictionary:

1. You define an empty dictionary.
2. You define the header of the for loop.
3. You assign a value to a key in the dictionary inside the body of the for loop.

Again, it looks like this:

```
d = {}
for key, value in some_iterable:
    k = get_key(key)
    v = get_value(value)
    d[k] = v
```

Again, if your keys and values are the same as the elements in the iterable, then you can just build the dictionary using **dict(some_iterable)**.

`get_key` and `get_value` just represent some transformation that you are making to the key and the value that you extract from the iterable, they aren't any particular function. Here's how we turn the traditional `for` loop form into a *dict comprehension*:

```
d = {get_key(key): get_value(value) for key, value in
 some_iterable}
```

2.4.3 `while` Statement

The `while` statement is suitable when you want to have repeated execution while an expression is `True`. Here's the generic form of the `while`:

```
while expression:
    suite
else:
    suite
```

If the expression evaluates to `False` (which can happen the first time it's evaluated), then the suite in the `else` statement, if present, is executed.

Let's see a simple example (write the following code in a file; I named mine *while.py*):

```
import random

counter = 0
while random.randint(0, 500) < 350:
    counter = counter + 1
print(counter)
```

(file while.py)

A quick explanation about the two new things here: **import** and `random`. The statement **import** allows you to import and load a module and use whatever that module provides: functions, constants, classes, etc. In section 2.7 *Modules and Packages*, I'll give a more thorough explanation, with lots of examples. `random` is a module that provides random variable generators. If you want to know more about this module, go to the interactive shell and enter the following commands:

```
>>> import random
>>> help(random)
>>> dir(random)
>>> help(random.randint)
```

The second command will give you a description of what the module is and what functionality it provides. The third command displays all the functions, classes and constants defined in the module. The last command is similar to **help(str.join)** or **help(list.append)**: it displays help on the method **randint**.

So, as you can see in the help screen, **randint** generates a random integer in a certain range `[a,  b]`, including the endpoints. Which means that every time you invoke **random.randint(0, 500)** it will return, hopefully, a different integer within that range. Let's now dissect the script with the `while` statement:

```
while random.randint(0, 500) < 350:
    counter = counter + 1
```

The expression `counter = counter + 1` is incrementing the value of `counter` of 1. It will be executed as long as the random integer generated is smaller than 350. But since it's supposed to be a random integer, you don't exactly know when will this expression evaluate to `False` and exit the `while` loop. That's why every time you run this script, it will print a different `counter`.

Note: another way of writing the expression `counter = counter + 1` is `counter += 1`.

This is valid for most operators when the variable occurs both on left and right hand side of the assignment. Here are other examples:

- `counter = counter * 2` is the same as `counter *= 2` (counter's new value is twice the old one)
- `counter = counter / 2` is the same as `counter /= 2` (the same for division)
- `string = string + string2` is the same as `string += string2` (it also works for string concatenation)

This also applies to bitwise operations.

2.4.4 `break` and `continue`

`break` and `continue` can only occur nested in a `for` or `while` loop. They are often part of the suite in an `if-else` statement, but this **must** occur in the scope of the loop.

Both `break` and `continue` change the normal flow of execution of a loop, where `break` terminates the execution of the nearest enclosing loop and `continue` forces the nearest enclosing loop to skip to the next iteration.

```
>>> for i in range(10):
...     if i > 3:
...         break
...     else:
...         print(i)
...
0
1
2
3
```

If `i` is not greater than 3, then it simply prints its value. When the comparison evaluates to `True`, the nearest enclosed loop (in this case, there is only one) is terminated. Let's see how it works with `continue`:

```
>>> for i in range(10):
...     if not i % 2:
...         continue
...     else:
...         print(i)
...
1
3
5
7
9
```

If `i` is an even number, it skips to the next value returned by **range** and the code that comes afterwards (**print(i)**) is ignored. How will `break` and `continue` behave in nested loops?

```
>>> for i in range(5):
...     for j in range(10, 19):
...         if j > 15:
...             break
...         else:
...             print(j)
...
10
11
12
13
14
15
10
(continues)
```

Without the `break` statement, this code would print *5* times (outer `for` loop) the numbers from *10* to *18* (inner `for` loop). Note that you don't really need to have the `else` there. You could simply put the **print** at the same level of indentation as the `if`, since after the `break` the rest of the code is skipped.

```
>>> for i in range(5):
...     for j in range(10, 19):
...         if j > 15:
```

```
...                break
...            print(j)
...
```

So the `break` statement is only affecting the execution of the inner `for` loop, which is the nearest enclosing loop. Here's an example with `continue`:

```
>>> for i in range(5):
...     for j in range(10, 19):
...         if not j % 2:
...             continue
...         print(j)
...
11
13
15
17
11
13
(continues)
```

The `continue` statement affects the normal flow of the inner `for` loop, by skipping to the next item in the iteration every time the current item is an even number. This code will print *5* times all the odd numbers between *10* and *19* (excluding the *19*).

Note: unlike certain programming languages, Python doesn't allow you to exit the outermost loop in nested loops using `break` in the innermost loops.

2.4.5 Functions

Functions are actually another data type, but they also control the flow of execution of your programs. Functions are a *callable* data type, because the *call* operator can be applied. Before going into more theory, let's see some examples:

```
>>> def print_hello():
...     print("Hello")
...
>>> print_hello()
Hello
```

In this code, I'm defining a function called **print_hello**, which doesn't expect any argument. This function definition **doesn't** execute the body. The execution of the body of the function only happens when the function is called, and you do so by typing the name of the function followed by opening and closing parentheses: **print_hello()**. In fact, the function definition is binding the function name (in the current local *namespace*) to a function object. We'll see in section *2.4.5.7* what a *namespace* is.

This function doesn't do anything special, but we're just warming up. Let's say that you want to define a function that takes any number as an argument and *returns* its square multiplied by two:

```
>>> def square_times_two(x):
...     return x**2 * 2
...
>>> square_times_two(2)
8
>>> square_times_two(3)
18
```

In the function definition, the parameter x indicates that the function expects exactly one argument when invoked.

Note: it may seem that I use the terms *argument* and *parameter* interchangeably, but it actually depends on the context. A *parameter* is a name used in a function definition, whereas an *argument* is the exact value you pass to the function invocation.
So if you have def func(x): ..., x is a *parameter*. When you invoke **func(2)**, 2 is an *argument*.

Whatever value you pass when you invoke the function will be replaced in every occurrence of x in the function body. Note that the body of the function is treating x as being an integer. No type check is being made, which means that if you provide an argument other than a number, this will fail and an exception will be raised:

```
>>> square_times_two("Hello")
Traceback (most recent call last):
 File "<stdin>", line 1, in <module>
 File "<stdin>", line 2, in square_times_two
TypeError: unsupported operand type(s) for ** or pow():
'str' and 'int'
```

Another important thing to note is the return statement. return statements may only occur nested in a function definition and it has the following form:

```
return [expression_list]
```

The square brackets indicate that expression_list is optional. In case expression_list is present, it will be evaluated and used as a *return value*, or else None will be implicitly used instead. The type of the value(s) returned determines, obviously, the return type of the function.

```
>>> a = print_hello()
Hello
>>> a is None
True
>>> type(a)
<class 'NoneType'>
```

The string Hello is being printed because that's what the function body is doing, but since the function doesn't return anything, the variable a is assigned the value None.

```
>>> a = square_times_two(3)
>>> a
18
```

On the other hand, the function **square_times_two** has a `return` statement followed by an expression, which evaluates to an integer and is returned.

Let's now define a function that expects two integers and returns the square of their sum:

```
>>> def square_sum(x, y):
...     return (x + y)**2
...
>>> square_sum(2, 3)
25
```

Now, this function definition has two parameters, x and y. The order of the arguments you specify when invoking the function will matter. This rule is pretty similar to the one applied to functions we learn in Math in school.

Let's now see what happens when you provide a number of arguments that is different from the one expected in the function definition:

```
>>> square_sum(2, 3, 4)
Traceback (most recent call last):
  File "<stdin>", line 1, in <module>
TypeError: square_sum() takes 2 positional arguments
but 3 were given
>>> square_sum(2)
Traceback (most recent call last):
  File "<stdin>", line 1, in <module>
TypeError: square_sum() missing 1 required positional
argument: 'y'
```

Quite expectable. You may have noticed that in the *exception* message it was mentioned *positional argument*. This is my cue to introduce you to the next topic, so continue reading!

2.4.5.1 Positional arguments

So far, the arguments we've been providing when calling functions are *positional arguments*. The way they are assigned to the variables in the function body depend on their position in the call expression. Nothing new here. The cool thing is that we can take advantage of *iterables* to provide positional arguments to functions, by preceding an *iterable* by *. This is called *unpacking*.

```
>>> def square_sum(x, y):
...     return (x + y)**2
...
>>> coordinates = [2, 3]
>>> square_sum(*coordinates)
25
>>> square_sum(*[2, 3])
25
```

When you *unpack*, the elements of the *iterable* will be used as *positional arguments* following the order at which they appear in the *iterable*. So the example above is the same as invoking **square_sum(2, 3)**.

Let's see a more complex example, where a user is expected to enter the coordinates, x and y, of two points separated by an empty space character. This will be passed to a function that calculates and returns the distance between those two points.

Sample input: 2 -3 7 14
Sample output: The distance is 17.72004514666935

In the sample input, 2 and -3 are *x* and *y* coordinates of the first point, and 7 and 14 are the *x* and *y* coordinates of the second point.

Let's see a possible solution for this little problem:

```python
import math

def distance(x1, y1, x2, y2):
    """
    Calculates and returns the distance between two
    points in a plane.
    :type x1: float
    :type y1: float
    :type x2: float
    :type y2: float
    :rtype: float
    """
    return math.sqrt((x2-x1)**2 + (y2-y1)**2)

coordinates = input("(x1 y1 x2 y2) ")
coordinates = [float(c) for c in coordinates.split(" ")]
d = distance(*coordinates)
print("The distance is {}".format(d))
```

(file distance.py)

And now we run the script:

```
➜  ~/StartCareerPython python distance.py
(x1 y1 x2 y2) 2 -3 7 14
The distance is 17.72004514666935
```

How did I get this solution? Let me explain my reasoning behind it with some backtracking.

We are interested in printing the distance between two points, which is given by a certain formula expressed in a certain function, which we'll call **distance**. The function distance expects four coordinates and returns a number:

```
d = distance(*coordinates)
print("The distance is {}".format(d))
```
(file distance.py)

If we run this script, it will fail miserably because we don't have **distance** nor `coordinates` defined. Let's start by the easiest one: `coordinates`.

```
coordinates = input("(x1 y1 x2 y2) ")
d = distance(*coordinates)
print("The distance is {}".format(d))
```
(file distance.py)

Like you've seen already, the **input** function returns a single string with whatever you pass to the *standard input* (your keyboard). The string argument that I am passing to **input** won't have any impact on the string. I am just using it to help whoever is running this script, so that they know the format of the expected input.

In order for this script to not fail, we need to have **distance** defined, right? So let's define it.

```
import math

def distance(x1, y1, x2, y2):
    return math.sqrt((x2-x1)**2 + (y2-y1)**2)

coordinates = input("(x1 y1 x2 y2) ")
d = distance(*coordinates)
print("The distance is {}".format(d))
```

I knew that I wanted my **distance** function to *return* a number based on a certain formula. That formula expects four numbers, which make up two coordinates. Also, there is a built-in module `math` that has a function **sqrt** that calculates the square root () of a number.

Now, if someone is using my distance function for some reason, they wouldn't know the type of the parameters of the function, right? Perhaps it's better to add a comment to the function...

```
import math

def distance(x1, y1, x2, y2):
    """
    Calculates and returns the distance between two
    points in a plane.
    :type x1: float
    :type y1: float
    :type x2: float
    :type y2: float
    :rtype: float
    """
    return math.sqrt((x2-x1)**2 + (y2-y1)**2)

coordinates = input("(x1 y1 x2 y2) ")
d = distance(*coordinates)
print("The distance is {}".format(d))
```

This function is quite simple and self-explanatory, so I don't need to explain what each parameter is. But I described the expected type of each parameter, nonetheless, because I could have written the function in such a way that it would expect strings as arguments instead and do the conversion to float inside its body.

Alright, we already have our function defined, but is the script ready? Let's see:

```
➜  ~/StartCareerPython python test.py
(x1 y1 x2 y2) 2 -3 7 14
Traceback (most recent call last):
  File "test.py", line 16, in <module>
    d = distance(*coordinates)
TypeError: distance() takes 4 positional arguments but
9 were given
```

We have a complain on line **16**, which is where we are unpacking `coordinates`. Ooops, it's still a single string! Even though a string is *unpackable*, this will not work because its characters won't translate into the type of coordinates we want.

We should have a list of *floats*, instead... How can we do it? Oh yes, we can actually **split** the string using a space as a delimiter, right?

```python
import math

def distance(x1, y1, x2, y2):
    """
    Calculates and returns the distance between two
    points in a plane.
    :type x1: float
    :type y1: float
    :type x2: float
    :type y2: float
    :rtype: float
    """
    return math.sqrt((x2-x1)**2 + (y2-y1)**2)

coordinates = input("(x1 y1 x2 y2) ")
coordinates = coordinates.split(" ")
d = distance(*coordinates)
print("The distance is {}".format(d))
```

It's looking better! Let's run one more time:

```
→ ~/StartCareerPython python test.py
(x1 y1 x2 y2) 2 -3 7 14
Traceback (most recent call last):
 File "test.py", line 17, in <module>
   d = distance(*coordinates)
 File "test.py", line 13, in distance
   return math.sqrt((x2-x1)**2 + (y2-y1)**2)
TypeError: unsupported operand type(s) for -: 'str' and
'str'
```

So the problem is that our `coordinates` variable is holding a list with strings, not floats. When we pass these strings to distance by *unpacking* `coordinates`, the function tries to apply the operand - to the strings (*str*), which is not supported.

Let's then create a list of floats, instead. We just need to grab each of the strings in the list returned by **split** and turn them into floats. We can either use a traditional `for` loop to build the new list or we can use a *list comprehension*. Let's go for the latter:

```python
import math

def distance(x1, y1, x2, y2):
    """
    Calculates and returns the distance between two
    points in a plane.
    :type x1: float
    :type y1: float
    :type x2: float
    :type y2: float
    :rtype: float
    """
    return math.sqrt((x2-x1)**2 + (y2-y1)**2)

coordinates = input("(x1 y1 x2 y2) ")
coordinates = [float(c) for c in coordinates.split(" ")]
d = distance(*coordinates)
print("The distance is {}".format(d))
```

Let's run the script one last time:

```
➜  ~/StartCareerPython python test.py
(x1 y1 x2 y2) 2 -3 7 14
17.72004514666935
```

Voilà!

Question: can you make the necessary changes in the code to use a *tuple* instead of a *list* of coordinates?

2.4.5.2 *Keyword arguments*

You've already seen a couple of *keyword arguments* before, for example `reverse` in the **sorted** function or `end` in **print**. *keyword arguments* are preceded by an identifier when the function is called. In this way, the order of the parameters in the function definition doesn't have to match the order of the *keyword arguments*:

```
>>> def square_sum(x, y):
...     return (x+y)**2
...
>>> square_sum(x=2, y=3)
25
>>> square_sum(y=3, x=2)
25
```

As long as you use *keyword arguments*, the order doesn't really matter because the function call is indicating how to assign the values to the function variables.

The same way you can unpack an *iterable* and use its elements as positional arguments, you can also unpack a dictionary and use each key/value pair as *keyword arguments*. Note that when unpacking a dictionary, it must be preceded by ****** instead of *****.

```
>>> d = {"x": 2, "y": 3}
>>> square_sum(**d)
25
>>> square_sum(**{"x": 2, "y": 3})
25
```

Let's now change a bit the requirements of our previous challenge regarding the distance between two points. This time, your program should expect an input in the form `x1=value y1=value x2=value y2=value`. Actually, let's make it in such a way that the order doesn't matter at all.

Sample Input 1: `x1=2 y1=-3 x2=7 y2=14`
Sample Output 1: `The distance is 17.72004514666935`

Sample Input 2: `y2=14 y1=-3 x1=2 x2=7`
Sample Output 2: `The distance is 17.72004514666935`

Here is one of many ways to solve the challenge:

```python
import math

def distance(x1, y1, x2, y2):
    """
    Calculates and returns the distance between two
    points in a plane.
    :type x1: float
    :type y1: float
    :type x2: float
    :type y2: float
    :rtype: float
    """
    return math.sqrt((x2-x1)**2 + (y2-y1)**2)

coordinates = input("> ")
coordinates = coordinates.split(" ")
coordinates = [c.split("=") for c in coordinates]
coordinates = {k: float(v) for k, v in coordinates}
d = distance(**coordinates)
print("The distance is {}".format(d))
```

Now you try solving it using some backtracking. If you get stuck, read the following explanation.

The list comprehension is building a list where each element is a list with two strings. If this step was too quick, go to the interactive shell and do experiments. Start off by removing the list comprehension and **c.split("=")**:

```python
>>> coordinates = "x1=2 y1=-3 x2=7 y2=14"
>>> coordinates.split(" ")
['x1=2', 'y1=-3', 'x2=7', 'y2=14']
```

Since we still need to get rid of the =, we use a list comprehension where each element will be the result of calling **split("=")** on each of these strings:

```
>>> coordinates = [c.split("=") for c in
⌐coordinates.split(" ")]

>>> coordinates
[['x1', '2'], ['y1', '-3'], ['x2', '7'], ['y2', '14']]
```

We can now take advantage of *multi-assignment* to extract both the *key* and the *value* for our *dict comprehension*, since each element in coordinates is a list with two elements: the first element will be the key and the second element will be the value. But since the second element is a string, we must convert it to a float using **float()**.

```
>>> coordinates = {k: float(v) for k, v in coordinates}
>>> coordinates
{'x1': 2, 'x2': 7, 'y1': -3, 'y2': 14}
```

That's pretty much it!

2.4.5.3 Default parameter values
When defining functions, it's possible to define default values for certain parameters. This means that if you don't pass certain arguments to a function call, a default value will be bound to the parameter.

We've already seen this in use, for example, with the **print** built-in function: if you don't specify the parameter end, then a newline character is used by default.

Let's see how you define a function with default parameter values:

```
>>> def print_something(smt="Hello"):
...        print(smt)
```

```
...
>>> print_something()
Hello
>>> print_something("World!")
World!
```

Note that if you mix normal parameters with parameters with default values, you must first specify the normal parameters and then the ones with default values:

```
# Incorrect
def print_something(smt="Hello", name):
    print(smt + name)

# Correct
def print_something(name, smt="Hello"):
    print(smt + name)
```

2.4.5.4 Variable number of positional and keyword arguments

A way of dealing with excess of arguments is using the form `*identifier` (for positional arguments) or `**identifier` (for keyword arguments). Most of the times, you will see `*args` and `**kwargs`, but this is pure convention, as *args* and *kwargs* don't have any special meaning in Python.

When `*identifier` is present, it will be initialized to a tuple containing any excess of positional arguments:

```
>>> def func(*args):
...     print(args)
...
>>> func()
()
>>> func(1, 2, 3)
(1, 2, 3)
```

If you want to access individual arguments, you do so by indexing the tuple as you would normally do:

```
>>> def func(*args):
...     if len(args) > 1:
...         print(args[0])
...
>>> func("Hello", 2)
Hello
```

On the other hand, when `**identifier` is present, it will be initialized to a dictionary containing the keyword arguments:

```
>>> def func(**kwargs):
...     print(kwargs)
...
>>> func(param1=2, param2="Hello")
{'param1': 2, 'param2': 'Hello'}
>>> func()
{}
>>> func(1)
Traceback (most recent call last):
 File "<stdin>", line 1, in <module>
TypeError: func() takes 0 positional arguments but 1
was given
```

Note that after a `*identifier` the parameters must be *keyword parameters* and must only be passed as keyword arguments:

```
>>> def func(*args, param1):
...     print(args)
...     print(param1)
...
>>> func(param1=10)
()
10
>>> func(1)
Traceback (most recent call last):
 File "<stdin>", line 1, in <module>
TypeError: func() missing 1 required keyword-only
argument: 'param1'
```

2.4.5.5 Nested functions
You can also define a function inside another function:

```
def do_operation(x, y):
    def add_numbers(x, y):
        return x+y

    def concat(x, y):
        return "{}{}".format(x, y)

    if isinstance(x, int) and isinstance(y, int):
        return add_numbers(x, y)
    else:
        return concat(x, y)

print(do_operation(1, 4))
print(do_operation(1, "4"))
```

(file nested_functions.py)

```
→ ~/StartCareerPython python nested_functions.py
5
14
```

Note that both inner functions are not accessible if you try to call them outside **do_operations**. Go on, give it a try!

Right now you might be wondering why would you want to use nested functions. For now, I'll just ask you to trust that there are practical situations where this is quite handy. I will show this later when I introduce you to some fancy topics.

2.4.5.6 Recursive functions
Recursive functions are functions that call themselves inside their body. One of the most typical examples used to show off the beauty of recursive functions is the factorial of a non-negative integer: $n!$.

Note: if you don't know or don't remember, the factorial of a non-negative integer n is the product of all positive integers less than or equal to n. For example, 5! = 5×4×3×2×1. Also, note that 0!=1.

With what you've learned so far, here's one possible way to define the factorial function:

```
>>> def factorial(n):
...     fact = 1
...     for i in range(1, n+1):
...         fact *= i
...     return fact
...
>>> factorial(5)
120
```

Nothing special here, right? Now let's see the recursive version:

```
>>> def recursive_factorial(n):
...     if n == 0:
...         return 1
...     else:
...         return n * recursive_factorial(n-1)
...
>>> recursive_factorial(5)
120
```

The suite in the `if` clause is called the *base case* of the recursion. It guarantees that the function won't be calling itself indefinitely. The base case varies, depending on the problem you are trying to solve.

```
factorial(5) =
  5 * factorial(4) =
    5 * 4 * factorial(3) =
      5 * 4 * 3 * factorial(2) =
        5 * 4 * 3 * 2 * factorial(1) =
          5 * 4 * 3 * 2 * 1 * factorial(0) ← Base case returns 1
```

Implementing functions in a recursive way may come at a cost in many situations, due to the overhead of function calls. Nonetheless, even though its iterative counterpart may be more efficient in most of the cases, the truth is that for certain problems the recursive way is much more intuitive and can also be faster. And even if they are not faster, you can use *recursiveness* to build a prototype and later you can implement an iterative version, if necessary. Also, recursive solutions tend to be shorter and more elegant.

Ok, the recursive solution for factorial wasn't shorter, so here is my one-liner (but keep in mind what I've told you about one-liners):

```
>>> def recursive_factorial(n):
...     return 1 if n == 0 else \
...         n * recursive_factorial(n-1)
...
```

You can use backslashes (\) when you want a statement to span more than one line.

2.4.5.7 Names, Namespaces and Scopes

Before proceeding to the next section, there is some knowledge that you must acquire and, hopefully, master. Not only will it help you do more complex stuff, but will also put you one step closer to becoming an advanced Python programmer.

A *namespace* is a place where mappings between *names* and objects are stored. *Names* can refer to variables or functions, for example. So when you enter $x = 4$ in the interactive shell, you are binding the name x to an integer object whose value is 4. The same goes for when you define a function: you are binding the function name to a function object. Nothing new for you here, right?

A *scope*, on the other hand, is a text region in a Python program and determines whether a namespace is directly accessible or not. It basically influences the resolution of names by defining their visibility within a code block. Let's see what this means with a few examples:

```
x = 10

def print_x():
    x = 5
    print(x)

print_x()
```
(file namespaces.py)

```
➜ ~/StartCareerPython python namespaces.py
5
```

The variable x will be searched in the innermost scope, which is the body of the function **print_x**. A binding between x and 5 was created inside the function, in a *local* namespace for the function. The *local namespace of a function* is created when a function is called and deleted when a function returns or when a function raises an exception that is not handled inside the function itself.

Let's see what happens when we remove that binding:

```
x = 10

def print_x():
    print(x)

print_x()
```

```
➜ ~/StartCareerPython python namespaces.py
10
```

The name x is searched in the *local namespace* but it can't be found. Since there are no other enclosing functions, the next-to-last scope will be searched, which contains the names in the *global namespace* of the module.

The module's *global namespace* contains two bindings: x and `print_x`. Are there any other namespaces? Of course. Besides the *local namespace* of a function and the *global namespace of a module*, there is also the *built-ins namespace*. This is where names like **abs**, **print** or **len** are stored.

The *built-ins namespace* is accessible from every scope. The set of attributes of an object (which we'll see in section *2.8 Object Oriented Programming*) also forms a namespace.

Let's start playing with a bit more exotic examples.

```
x = 10

def outer_print_x():
    x = 7

    def inner_print_x():
        print(x)

    inner_print_x()

outer_print_x()
```
(file namespaces.py)

```
➜  ~/StartCareerPython python namespaces.py
7
```

This time I'm using nested functions just to illustrate names resolution. The name x is first searched in the innermost scope of function **inner_print_x**, but it can't be found. The nearest enclosing scope is the one of the function **outer_print_x**, which contains other names, including x. A `NameError` exception will be raised if a name can't be found at all.

The different namespaces that I've mentioned so far are created at different moments and have different life times. Like I've said, the local namespace for a function is created when the function is called and deleted when the function returns. The namespace for the built-in names is created when the Python interpreter starts up and it's never deleted. This happens either when you start the interactive shell or when you start the interpreter in another way (for example, executing a script in a file). The global namespace for a module is created when a module definition is read in.

When you are in the interactive shell, the statements you enter are being executed in a module called __main__. If you're not in the interactive shell, then go there and type __name__:

```
>>> __name__
'__main__'
```

__main__ is the scope in which top-level code executes. Besides when you are executing statements in the interactive shell, a module's name is also set to __main__ when the module is being read from the standard input or when it's being executed as a script.

Let's go a bit deeper in our experiments.

```
x = 10

def print_x():
    print(x)

if __name__ == "__main__":
    print_x()
```

(file namespaces.py)

```
→ ~/StartCareerPython python namespaces.py
10
```

The `if` statement is a common practice when writing Python programs: it allows a module to discover whether it's running in the main scope or not. If that's the case, then the *suite* in the `if` statement will be executed. If the module is being imported by another module, then it won't.

Write the following code in a file called *test_names.py*.

```
import namespaces

print("Hello")
```
(file test_names.py)

```
→ ~/StartCareerPython python test_names.py
Hello
```

The code in the new file is *importing* the file *namespaces.py* as a module. But since we have the `if` statement in *namespaces.py,* the function **print_x** is not called.

Now try to comment out the `if` statement and see what happens:

```
x = 10

def print_x():
    print(x)

#if __name__ == "__main__":
print_x()
```
(file namespaces.py)

```
→ ~/StartCareerPython python test_names.py
10
Hello
```

print_x is called first, since the `import` statement is the very first statement in *test_names.py*. After that, whatever code comes after the `import` will be executed.

You can now uncomment the if statement. Let's try to call **print_x** from *test_names.py*:

```
import namespaces

namespaces.print_x()
```
(file test_names.py)

```
→ ~/StartCareerPython python test_names.py
10
```

Awesome, right? Even though the function **print_x** is being called from *test_names.py*, it still prints the value of x. This is because no matter where you are calling the function from, the global namespace of a function defined in a module is that module's namespace. You can confirm this by changing both *namespaces.py* and *test_names.py*:

```
def print_x():
    print(x)

if __name__ == "__main__":
    print_x()
```
(file namespaces.py)

```
import namespaces

x = 10

namespaces.print_x()
```
(file test_names.py)

```
→ ~/StartCareerPython python test_names.py
Traceback (most recent call last):
```

```
  File "test_names.py", line 5, in <module>
    namespaces.print_x()
  File "/Users/pmpro/StartCareerPython/namespaces.py",
line 2, in print_x
    print(x)
NameError: name 'x' is not defined
```

Of course one can always argue that x is being defined after the `import`, so let's define it before:

```
x = 10

import namespaces

namespaces.print_x()
```

(file test_names.py)

```
➜ ~/StartCareerPython python test_names.py
Traceback (most recent call last):
  File "test_names.py", line 5, in <module>
    namespaces.print_x()
  File "/Users/pmpro/StartCareerPython/namespaces.py",
line 2, in print_x
    print(x)
NameError: name 'x' is not defined
```

No, it doesn't really matter: the global namespace of the module where the function was defined doesn't have the name x.

We're almost done! One other thing to keep in mind is that namespaces prevent name collision, which means that you can have the same name defined in different namespaces without a problem.

Do you remember the function **randint** from the module *random*? Alright, let's change yet again our file *namespaces.py*:

```
import random

def print_x():
    print(x)
```

```
def randint():
    return "This is my randint"

if __name__ == "__main__":
    print(randint())
    print(random.randint(0, 5))
```

```
→ ~/StartCareerPython python namespaces.py
This is my randint
5
```

And we're done with *namespaces* and *scopes*! Some details were left unwritten for now, because the objective is not to overwhelm you with information. I would suggest you to make as many experiments as possible, so that you can have a better understanding of how names resolution works.

2.5 Handling Files

Behold the files! Such a simple name and yet powerful abstraction. They can hold images, as well as love letters. They can be a virus that will do evil stuff to your computer or a dear *mp3* that you listen to if you aren't much of a fan of Internet radio.

At the end of the day, what determines what your file is, is the program that interprets its contents, as well as how structured is the content of the file.

In modern Operating Systems, files are organized into one-dimensional arrays of bytes. Even without specifying the file extension (*.py*, *.jpg* or *.mp3*), a program can successfully execute its contents and provide the desired outcome, as long as it makes the right assumption. For example, if you rename the file *namespaces.py* to *namespaces.jpg*, you can still run the script in the command line, but the same won't happen if you rename an image to *whatever.py*. All the non-beginners reading this are rolling their eyes and calling me "Captain Obvious". Come on, bear with me!

So, what makes a PDF a PDF and not a JPEG? Or an MP3? Well, these (and other) files often have internal *metadata*, which is information that is always placed in the same specific location and identifies the file type. This information can be a binary string, for example.

Let's get our hands dirty and start playing with some files! Before you can change the contents of a file, you must **open** it.

```
>>> f = open('somefile.pdf')
>>> type(f)
<class '_io.TextIOWrapper'>
```

I have a PDF file called *somefile.pdf* in the directory where I started my Python interactive shell. If you have any PDF file (which I believe you do), copy it to the directory where you are starting your interactive shell and replace *somefile.pdf* with whatever name your file has.

With only one argument, the function will open the file in *read text mode*. When you check the type, it says _io.TextIOWrapper. The function **open** returns a *file object*, but in fact you have 3 categories of *file objects*: *raw binary files*, *buffered binary files* and *text files*. It all depends on how you open a file. You can check the methods supported by this file object, by typing **dir(f)**.

When you are done working with the file, you can **close** it:

```
>>> f.close()
>>>
```

2.5.1 Reading from files

Opening and closing files is not interesting if you don't do anything with their contents, so let's start by reading the contents of a file! I created a regular text file (which I named *somefile.txt*, for the sake of originality) in the same directory and filled it with the following content:

```
This is one line.
This is another line.
And yet another one.
```

> **Note**: because you should be all command-line now, it's important that you get acquainted with the most common commands. If you want to check the contents of a file in the command line, you can use `cat`:
>
> ```
> ➜ ~/StartCareerPython cat somefile.txt
> This is one line.
> This is another line.
> And yet another one.
> ```
>
> If the file is expected to be too long, you can use `|  more` after `cat`, like `cat somefile.txt | more`:
>
> ```
> This is a big text file.
> I will just copy past the lines.
> Because I am too lazy to think of more text.
> This is a big text file.
> I will just copy past the lines.
> :
> ```
>
> You will notice that the console will change slightly, by placing a colon at the bottom. This is a way of saying that there is more text and you should use the cursor to move up and down (up and down arrow keys). The | is called the *pipe* and allows you to pass the output of `cat` to the command `more`. To quit `more` just type q.

Let's now create a little Python script called *read_files.py* and write some code in it:

```
f = open("somefile.txt")
for line in f:
    print(line)
```

```
f.close()
```
(file read_files.py)

```
→ ~/StartCareerPython python read_files.py
This is one line.

This is another line.

And yet another one.
```

There seems to be an extra newline between each line of our file. This is because each line in the file already has a newline character (because we implicitly added it) and the function **print** terminates with a newline by default.

We can solve this in two ways (ok, maybe more): we either tell **print** to terminate with an empty string or remove the newline character from each line we print.

```
f = open("somefile.txt")
for line in f:
    print(line, end="")

f.close()
```
(file read_files.py)

```
f = open("somefile.txt")
for line in f:
    print(line.strip())

f.close()
```

Both ways will provide the same output:

```
→ ~/StartCareerPython python read_files.py
This is one line.
This is another line.
And yet another one.
```

The reason why we are able to pass the file object f to the for loop is because the object is *iterable*. You can confirm this by typing **dir(f)** and verifying that the object implements the method **__iter__**. The current item on each iteration will be a different line of the file.

Is there any other way of reading the contents of the file? Yes, there is. You can use, for example, the methods **readline** and **readlines**. The method **readline** reads and returns a line from the file. When the end of the file is reached (EOF), an empty string is returned instead:

```
f = open("somefile.txt")
line = f.readline()
while line:
    print(line.strip())
    line = f.readline()

f.close()
```

But this code looks quite ugly, right? Let's make it prettier:

```
f = open("somefile.txt")
while True:
    line = f.readline()
    if not line:
        break
    print(line.strip())

f.close()
```

If you see the documentation of the method, you will see that actually there is a parameter called size (defaults to -1 if not specified) which allows you to indicate how many bytes you want to read.

Let's modify our file and see how it works:

```
f = open("somefile.txt")
while True:
```

```
    line = f.readline(5)
    if not line:
        break
    print(line)

f.close()
```

The argument passed to the method **readline** indicates that we want to read 5 bytes at a time, which corresponds to 5 ASCII characters in our text file. I removed the **strip** call for each line, so that you can have a visual understanding on how the size argument affects the **readline**.

```
➜ ~/StartCareerPython python read_files.py
This
is on
e lin
e.

This
is an
other
line
.

And y
et an
other
one.
```

So, **readline** will read at most 5 bytes or until it finds a newline character. What about the method **readlines**? This method will read the entire file and return a list with the lines. Unless the file you are reading is small, this way of reading should be avoided, as you may run out of memory. Nonetheless, there is a parameter hint which works in a similar way as size does for **readline**.

So far, we've opened the file in *text mode*, which is the default. When opened in text mode, the methods that read from the file return string objects. We can also open the file in *binary mode* and the reading methods return *bytes* objects. Let's see how this can be achieved:

```
f = open("somefile.txt", "rb")
for line in f:
    print(line)

f.close()
```

(file read_files_binary.py)

```
→ ~/StartCareerPython python read_files_binary.py
b'This is one line.\n'
b'This is another line.\n'
b'And yet another one.\n'
```

This time, the iterator returns *bytes* objects. If you remember the section about the *bytes* data type, then you can make sense out of this output. If you don't, then go back to section *2.2.2.3 Bytes*.

Remember: bytes sequences hold 7-bit ASCII characters and any element that is an integer greater than 127 must be properly escaped.

As you may have noticed, I passed a string as a second argument to **open**. This string specifies the *mode* of opening a file. The first character, r, says that I want to open the file for reading and b says that I want to open it in binary mode. If b wasn't specified, it would default to text mode, which is the same as specifying t instead of b: f = open("somefile.txt", "rt"). The table below contains the available modes, as specified in the *official documentation*[14]:

Character	Meaning
'r'	Open for reading (default)
'w'	Open for writing, truncating the file first.

`'x'`	Open for exclusive creation, failing if the file already exists.
`'a'`	Open for writing, appending to the end of the file if it exists.
`'b'`	Binary mode
`'t'`	Text mode (default)
`'+'`	Open a disk file for updating (reading and writing)
`'U'`	Universal newlines mode (deprecated)

Make sure to check the official documentation of **open**[14] in the section *Built-in Functions* from the *Python Standard Library*.

> **Question 1**: let's go back to the PDF example at the beginning of section 2.5. Open it in read-only text mode and try print the first two lines. What happens? Now open it in read-only binary mode and try to print the first two lines. What happens? Did you spot the bytes that inform you that it's a PDF document?
>
> **Question 2**: how can you read a character in a specific position in the file without reading an entire line? **Hint**: seek.

2.5.2 Writing to files

Alright, we can open files and read their contents. What about writing data into a file? That's even better, right?

When you want to write data into a file, you have two possible scenarios: either the file exists already or it doesn't. Obvious. On the event of the file not existing, we are creating a new file. If the file exists already, we will either append the new data or we will be overwriting existing contents.

Let's explore these scenarios!

2.5.2.1 Creating a new file
Creating a new file is as simple as opening a file with a name that doesn't exist yet in `w` mode. You don't even need to write

anything to the file, you can just call **close** on the file object right away.

```
f = open("somefile2.txt", "w")
f.close()
```
(file write_files.py)

```
➜ ~/StartCareerPython python write_files.py
```

To confirm that the file exists already, enter the command `ls` in the directory where you executed the script. This lists the contents of the current directory.

Now let's modify a bit our script so that we can write data into the file:

```
f = open("somefile2.txt", "w")
f.write("This is some data.")
f.close()
```
(file write_files.py)

```
➜ ~/StartCareerPython python write_files.py
➜ ~/StartCareerPython cat somefile2.txt
This is some data.
```

Because we're opening the file in *text mode*, the argument of the **write** method is expected to be a string. If you try to write a *bytes* object, the method will raise a `TypeError` *exception*.

```
f = open("somefile2.txt", "w")
f.write(b"This is some data.")
f.close()
```
(file write_files.py)

```
→ ~/StartCareerPython python write_files.py
Traceback (most recent call last):
  File "write_files.py", line 2, in <module>
    f.write(b"This is some data.")
TypeError: write() argument must be str, not bytes
```

Then let's open the file in binary mode instead, but first delete it by entering the command `rm somefile2.txt` in the current directory.

```
f = open("somefile2.txt", "wb")
f.write(b"This is some data.")
f.close()
```
(file write_files.py)

```
→ ~/StartCareerPython cat somefile2.txt
This is some data.
```

> **Challenge**: the method **writelines** is the writing counterpart of **readlines**. Write a script that takes comma separated groups of integers and writes the sum of each group on a new line in a file. Use the method **writelines**.
>
> **Sample Input**: 18 14 2 0 99, 104 33 7 1 21, 257 90
> **Sample resulting file**:
> 133
> 166
> 347

2.5.2.2 Writing into an existing file

Now that we know how to create a file and add some data to it, let's see how can we add data to an existing file. We'll keep working on *somefile2.txt* for that effect, which right now should contain the string `This is some data.`.

```
f = open("somefile2.txt", "w")
f.write("This is a line in an existing file.")
f.close()
```
(file write_existing_files.py)

```
→ ~/StartCareerPython cat somefile2.txt
This is a line in an existing file.
```

The old content was replaced. If you recall the table with *opening modes*, then you'll remember that when using `w` the file will be opened for writing and truncated before (in case it already existed). If you want to append content to the file, then you must use `a` when opening it:

```
f = open("somefile2.txt", "a")
f.write("\nThis content was appended to the end of the
⌐file.")
f.close()
```
(file write_existing_files.py)

```
→ ~/StartCareerPython cat somefile2.txt
This is a line in an existing file.
This content was appended to the end of the file.
```

2.5.3 The `with` statement

Even though the `with` statement is often used when handling files, its usage goes far beyond. This powerful construct allows you to write cleaner and more advanced code and it does so by wrapping the execution of a code block with methods defined by a *context manager*.

The `with` statement is comparable in a way to a `for` loop, where you pass an *iterable* object to it and obtain an *iterator*. In the `with` statement, you pass a *context expression* that is evaluated to obtain a *context manager*.

Let's start by examining the structure of a `with` statement:

```
with with_item ("," with_item)* :
    suite
```

And `with_item` is something with the following form:

```
expression ["as" target]
```

This notation may seem a bit confusing, but in a few seconds it will make sense. The `()*` notation means that whatever exists inside the parentheses should occur zero or more times, in this case "`,`" `with_item`. Which means that a `with` statement can have one or more `with_item` separated by commas.

On the other hand, the `[]` notation in the `with_item` means that whatever is inside the square brackets is optional. Let's now see a practical example:

```python
with open("somefile2.txt"):
    print("Yay")
```
(file with_statement.py)

This `with` statement has one `with_item` without the "`as`" `target` optional part. It's not very interesting because we can't do anything with the file, and that's where `as target` enters:

```python
with open("somefile2.txt") as f:
    for line in f:
        print(line, end="")
```
(file with_statement.py)

```
→ ~/StartCareerPython python with_statement.py
This is a line in an existing file.
This content was appended to the end to the file.
```

That's more like it! Let's now see an example of a `with` statement with two `with_item`:

```
with open("somefile2.txt") as f1,
     open("somefile3.txt", "w") as f2:
    for line in f1:
        f2.write(line)
```
(file with_statement.py)

The code above copies the content of *somefile2.txt* to a new file *somefile3.txt*, line by line.

You may have noticed that I haven't called the method **close** in any file object so far. The `with` statement goes hand in hand with another data type: *context manager*.

Like I said before about the `for` statement, whatever object you pass must be an *iterable* and implement the **__iter__** method, which returns an iterator for that object.

In the `with` statement, the `expression` in the `with_item` is evaluated in order to obtain a *context manager*. If there is a `target` in the `with_item`, then the value returned when the `expression` is evaluated will be bound to `target`. The *context manager* implements two methods: **__enter__** and **__exit__**. These two methods basically wrap the execution of the suite in the `with` statement, meaning that when the *context manager* is obtained, its **__enter__** method is called. When the suite is executed, the **__exit__** method is invoked.

A file object is an example of a *context manager*: it implements an **__enter__** method that returns the file object itself and its **__exit__** method closes the file. That's the reason why we don't need to invoke close explicitly.

2.6 Handling Errors and Exceptions

When you write software, it will be used directly by people or by other software. Because no one is perfect, either your software will contain errors or will have to deal with errors that result from external factors, such as bad input, no network connection, etc.

That's where *Exceptions* come in: they break out the normal flow of a code block in order to handle errors or exceptional conditions. You've already seen a few exceptions in the examples above. For example, when you try to write a *bytes* object into a file that was opened in *text mode*, the **write** method will raise a `TypeError` *exception*.

2.6.1 `raise` statement

You can also raise exceptions in your code explicitly, in order to indicate that something went wrong, with a more "user friendly" message. Take the following code, which simply expects to receive a number as an input and prints its square:

```
number = input("Enter a number: ")
print(int(number)**2)
```

Now, if you pass something other than digits to the input, the function **int** will raise an exception:

```
→ ~/StartCareerPython python exceptions1.py
Enter a number: 1a
Traceback (most recent call last):
 File "exceptions1.py", line 2, in <module>
   print(int(number)**2)
ValueError: invalid literal for int() with base 10:
'1a'
```

You could also raise the exception yourself, with a custom message, like this:

```
number = input("Enter a number: ")
if not number.isnumeric():
```

```
    raise ValueError("You must enter a number!!!")
else:
    print(int(number)**2)
```

Note that you don't have to raise a `ValueError` exception, but you'll understand in a bit why the type of the exception actually matters. The `raise` statement has the following form:

```
raise [expression [from expression]]
```

The outer square brackets mean that `expression` is optional and the inner square brackets mean that `from expression` is optional on the event of passing the first `expression` to `raise`.

The first `expression` is evaluated as an exception object and `from expression` is used for *exception chaining*. Before explaining what *exception chaining* is, let me go back to the importance of exception types.

2.6.2 `try` statement

This is also my cue to make a sneaky introduction to a few concepts related to the section *2.8 Object Oriented Programming*. Don't worry if a couple of terms (like *inheritance* or *instance* or *subclass*) won't make much sense for you now.

Python has a bunch of built-in exceptions and they follow a hierarchy. At the top of the hierarchy of all built-in exceptions there is `BaseException`, which shouldn't be directly inherited from by your own exceptions when you build them. For that, you should use `Exception`, from which all built-in non-system-exiting inherit from. System-exiting exceptions (such as `KeyboardInterrupt` or `SystemExit`) allow the interpreter to exit.

Let's see:

```
>>> print(1/0)
Traceback (most recent call last):
  File "<stdin>", line 1, in <module>
ZeroDivisionError: division by zero
>>> z = ZeroDivisionError()
>>> isinstance(z, Exception)
True
>>> isinstance(z, BaseException)
True
```

The built-in function **isinstance** checks whether the first argument (which is any object) is an instance or subclass of the second argument, which is a class. So all the checks are `True` because `ZeroDivisionError` inherits from `Exception` which, in turn, inherits from `BaseException`.

But why does this matter? Because you may want to do something specific when a certain type of exception occurs. You may want to have *exception handlers* and you do this with a `try` statement:

```
while True:
    try:
        number = input("Enter a number: ")
        print(int(number)**2)
        break
    except ValueError:
        print("I asked for a number!!! Try again...")
```
(file exceptions1.py)

Take the example above. The code block between `try` and `except` can potentially raise an exception. The suite of the `except` is your *exception handler,* so when a `ValueError` exception occurs in the `try` suite, the code will print `I asked for a number!!! Try again...`.

When the `ValueError` exception is raised the normal flow of execution is broken, meaning that `break` is not executed because the flow jumps immediately to the exception handler.

Which in turn means that until you enter a number, this code will be executed in an infinite loop.

Let's now see how we can have different exception handlers for different types of exceptions.

```
while True:
    try:
        number = input("Enter a number: ")
        print(1/int(number))
        break
    except ValueError:
        print("I asked for a number!!! Try again...")
    except ZeroDivisionError:
        print("Don't enter 0 (zero).")
```
(file exceptions2.py)

If the user enters something other than a number, the flow of execution is broken and the first exception handler is executed (for `ValueError` exception). If the user enters a 0 (zero), the second exception handler is executed instead, for `ZeroDivisionError` exception.

```
→ ~/StartCareerPython python exceptions2.py
Enter a number: 0
Don't enter 0 (zero).
Enter a number: 1e
I asked for a number!!! Try again...
Enter a number: 14
0.07142857142857142
```

If you want a broader exception handler which is executed when any exception is raised, you can simply have an `except` clause without specifying the exception type:

```
while True:
    try:
        number = input("Enter a number: ")
        print(1/int(number))
        break
```

```
    except:
        print("Something went wrong...try again!")
```

(file exceptions3.py)

```
➜ ~/StartCareerPython python exceptions3.py
Enter a number: 0
Something went wrong...try again!
Enter a number: 1e
Something went wrong...try again!
Enter a number: 14
0.07142857142857142
```

The `try` statement can also have a `finally` clause, which contains code that will be executed no matter what. Let's see:

```
while True:
    try:
        number = input("Enter a number: ")
        print(1/int(number))
        break
    except ValueError:
        print("I asked for a number!!! Try again...")
    except ZeroDivisionError:
        print("Don't enter 0 (zero).")
    finally:
        print("This is always printed")
```

```
➜ ~/StartCareerPython python exceptions3.py
Enter a number: 0
Don't enter 0 (zero).
This is always printed
Enter a number: 1e
I asked for a number!!! Try again...
This is always printed
Enter a number: 14
0.07142857142857142
This is always printed
```

This means that if no exception occurs in your code, the exception handlers won't be executed at all but the code in the `finally` clause will be.

The `try` statement can also have an `else` clause, whose suite is executed if and when the control flows off the `try` clause.

```
while True:
    try:
        number = input("Enter a number: ")
        print(int(number)**2)
    except ValueError:
        print("I asked for a number!!! Try again...")
    else:
        print("Awesome!")
        break
    finally:
        print("This is always printed")
```

(file exceptions4.py)

```
→ ~/StartCareerPython python exceptions4.py
Enter a number: 1e
I asked for a number!!! Try again...
This is always printed
Enter a number: 14
196
Awesome!
This is always printed
```

Note that if the `break` statement was part of the `try` clause, then the `else` suite wouldn't be executed.
You can also assign the exception object to a variable:

```
while True:
    try:
        number = input("Enter a number: ")
        print(int(number)**2)
        break
    except ValueError as exc:
        print("I asked for a number!!!
⏎[{}]".format(exc))
```

(file exceptions5.py)

```
➔ ~/StartCareerPython python exceptions5.py
Enter a number: 1e
I asked for a number!!! [invalid literal for int() with
base 10: '1e']
```

I didn't cover everything there is about Exception Handling, but this was exhaustive enough. Make sure you read the official documentation about:

- The `try` statement[15], from *Python Language Reference*.
- The `raise` statement[16], also from *Python Language Reference*.
- *Built-in Exceptions*[17], from *Python Standard Library*.
- *Errors and Exceptions*[18], from *Python Tutorial*.

2.7 Modules and Packages

As you progress and start writing longer and more complex software, the necessity of splitting code in several files will arise.

Having your program split in several files will make it easier for you to maintain it, as well as for other people to collaborate on the project you're working on. But one of the most interesting aspects is code reusability, meaning that you can have function or class definitions written in one place and reuse them across your entire application (or even other applications) without ever having to do copy paste.

In Python, a *module* is a file with code that contains definitions and statements. The name of the *module* will be the name of the file without the extension. Which means if you have a file *something.py* with a bunch of function definitions, it can be used as a module whose name is `something`.

In Python, programs are structured as *packages* and *modules*. A *package* is a directory that must contain a special file called __init__.py, that contains the initialization code for that package. Even though this file can be empty, it MUST exist for a directory to be treated as package. A package can contain other packages alongside with modules.

Let's get our hands dirty!

2.7.1 The `import` statement revisited

Let's start by creating a file called *module1.py* with a couple of definitions:

```
def add2(x):
    return x + 2

def add3(x):
    return x + 3
```

(file module1.py)

Now open the interactive shell in the same directory and enter the following:

```
>>> import module1
```

Note that this is not creating bindings of the names in the module in the current namespace. You can confirm that by entering **dir()**:

```
>>> dir()
['__builtins__', '__cached__', '__doc__', '__loader__',
'__name__', '__package__', '__spec__', 'module1']
```

You can also check the names that module1 defines, by entering **dir(module1)**. Just like with math or random, if you want to use the functions defined in the module you must precede the name of the function with the name of the module and a dot:

```
>>> module1.add2(5)
7
```

Now quit the interactive shell and start it again. Instead of using the previous form of import, we will explore others. For example, let's import just one name from our module:

```
>>> from module1 import add2
>>> dir()
['__builtins__', '__cached__', '__doc__', '__loader__',
'__name__', '__package__', '__spec__', 'add2']
```

This way of importing creates a binding in the current namespace, in this case of the function **add2**. Which means that you don't need to precede **add2** with anything else when using it:

```
>>> add2(6)
8
```

Another way of creating bindings in the current namespace by importing all the names from a module is as follows (quit and start the interactive shell):

```
>>> from module1 import *
>>> dir()
['__builtins__', '__cached__', '__doc__', '__loader__',
'__name__', '__package__', '__spec__', 'add2', 'add3']
```

This won't import any name starting with one underscore. If your module has too many definitions and you are only interested in a few of them, you can cherry pick the names you want to import.

Let's first add another definition to our module:

```
def add2(x):
    return x + 2

def add3(x):
    return x + 3

def sum_squares(x, y):
    return x**2 + y**2
```
(file module1.py)

If you just need **add2** and **sum_squares**, you can import them as follows:

```
>>> from module1 import add2, sum_squares
>>> dir()
['__builtins__', '__cached__', '__doc__', '__loader__',
'__name__', '__package__', '__spec__', 'add2',
'sum_squares']
```

You can even import a module or a name using an *alias*:

```
>>> import module1 as mymodule
>>> dir()
['__builtins__', '__cached__', '__doc__', '__loader__',
'__name__', '__package__', '__spec__', 'mymodule']
>>> from module1 import sum_squares as sumsquares
>>> sumsquares(2, 3)
13
```

2.7.2 Packages

Modules are a great way of avoiding naming conflicts due to namespace independence and also a way of promoting code reusability.

Packages, on the other hand, help you structure your modules namespaces. Like I said before, packages are directories that contain a special file *__init__.py*, which contains code for initializing the package. The file can be empty, but it must exist in order for the directory to be treated as a package.

Let's say that you want to develop a Chat application, which allows the users to send and receive various types of messages, like text, audio or video. A possible structure of your program would be as follows:

```
chat/                    # Top-level package
    __init__.py          # Initialize the chat package
    message/             # Subpackage for messages related stuff
        __init__.py          # Initialize messages subpackage
        formats/             # Subpackage for message formats
            __init__.py          # Initialize subpackage
            text.py
            audio.py
            video.py

    user.py
    room.py
    server.py
```

(package structure)

chat, message and formats are directories turned into packages.

Packages organize modules namespaces with dots, so when you want to refer to the module text from message formats, you do it like chat.message.formats.text .

Let's create a fake structure just to play around with packages for a bit:

```
➜  ~/StartCareerPython mkdir -p chat/message/formats

➜  ~/StartCareerPython touch chat/__init__.py \
> chat/message/__init__.py \
> chat/message/formats/__init__.py \
> chat/message/formats/text.py

➜  ~/StartCareerPython tree chat/
chat/
├── __init__.py
```

```
└─ message
   ├─ __init__.py
   └─ formats
      ├─ __init__.py
      └─ text.py

2 directories, 4 files
```

Just a couple of notes here:

- `mkdir -p` will create the intermediate directories as required. If I had just entered `mkdir chat/message/formats` it would generate an error because `chat` and `chat/message` didn't exist before.

- `touch` changes a file's access and modification times. If the file doesn't exist, it creates an empty file with the specified name, which is what I am interested in. It's more practical than opening an editor and saving an empty file. The \ can also be used in the command-line, for commands that span more than one line.

Let's now add a function definition to *text.py* ...

```
def filter_message(text):
    print("Function that filters messages.")
```
(file chat/message/formats/text.py)

...and start the interactive shell in the directory where you created the `chat` package. Let's import the `text` module and call the function **filter_message**:

```
>>> import chat.message.formats.text
>>> chat.message.formats.text.filter_message("Test")
Function that filters messages.
```

It's not very practical, because you have to write huge amounts of text just to use a function. Instead, we can use the `from … import *` format:

```
>>> from chat.message.formats import text
>>> text.filter_message("Test")
Function that filters messages.
```

Much better, right? And to close this section, let's see how can we execute a module as a script. Quit the interactive shell and create the file chat/server.py:

```
→ ~/StartCareerPython touch chat/server.py
```

And now let's add just some fake functions to illustrate the example:

```
def start_server():
    print("Starting chat server.")

if __name__ == "__main__":
    start_server()
```
(file chat/server.py)

And now if you want to run your *server* module as a script, you can just do it as follows:

```
→ ~/StartCareerPython python chat/server.py
Starting chat server.
```

Of course, assuming your current directory is the one where you created the `chat` package.

Nonetheless, this won't work if you are importing your own modules from your code. Let's change *server.py* a bit by importing `text` module from message formats:

```
import chat.message.formats.text

def start_server():
    print("Starting chat server.")

if __name__ == "__main__":
    start_server()
```

(file chat/server.py)

And now we try to run as before:

```
➜  ~/StartCareerPython python chat/server.py
Traceback (most recent call last):
 File "chat/server.py", line 1, in <module>
    import chat.message.formats.text
ImportError: No module named 'chat'
```

Ooops! Why did this happen? It has got to do with the way modules are found when they are imported. When a module is imported, it is first searched in the built-in modules. Because there is no such module in the built-ins, a directory called chat will be searched in the list of directories given by the variable sys.path. path is a variable from the built-in module sys and is initialized from:

- The directory containing the input script (in this case **chat/**)
- PYTHONPATH[19], which is the *environment variable* that contains a list of directory names in order to augment the default search path for modules.
- The installation-dependent default search path.

Basically, sys.path holds a bunch of locations where imported modules and packages are searched in case they are not built-in.

If you pay attention to the first point, you'd see that sys.path is initialized from the directory containing the input script. Which means, that our import would work if inside the directory **chat/** there would be another directory `chat` with `message` and `formats` subdirectories.

It would also work if instead of importing `chat.message.formats.text` we would just import `message.formats.text`.

```
import message.formats.text

def start_server():
    print("Starting chat server.")

if __name__ == "__main__":
    start_server()
```
(file chat/server.py modified)

```
➜ ~/StartCareerPython python chat/server.py
Starting chat server.
```

But this is not what we are interested in, or else our imports would all have to be *relative*, and thus losing expressiveness.

The best way is to use the −m flag when invoking the interpreter and pass directly the module `chat.server` as an argument. First, put the import in *server.py* back the way it was. And then run the command from the top directory, where you have the **chat/**:

```
➜ ~/StartCareerPython python −m chat.server
Starting chat server.
```

If you want to see what does the −m flag do, type `man python`. This will take you the Python's interpreter manual page. Move up and down with the up and down *arrow keys*, or navigate page by page by pressing the *spacebar*. To quit, simply press *q*.

Make sure you go check *Modules*[20] chapter in the tutorial from the official documentation. Also consider reading the section about the `import` *statement*[21] from Python Language Reference.

2.7.3 A note on `import`

Something to take into consideration is that any defined names starting with one single underscore won't be imported when using the form `from <module-name> import *`. Let's see an example:

```
def _add2(x):
    return x+2

def sum_squares(x, y):
    return x**2 + y**2
```
(file modules2.py)

```
>>> from module2 import *
>>> dir()
['__builtins__', '__cached__', '__doc__', '__loader__',
'__name__', '__package__', '__spec__', 'sum_squares']
```

Only **sum_squares** was imported, not the **_add2**. As a side note, the underscore character, when using the interactive shell, holds the result of the last evaluation:

```
>>> x + 2
4
>>> _
4
>>> dir()
['__builtins__', '__cached__', '__doc__', '__loader__',
'__name__', '__package__', '__spec__', 'sum_squares',
'x']
>>> _
['__builtins__', '__cached__', '__doc__', '__loader__',
```

```
'__name__', '__package__', '__spec__', 'sum_squares',
'x']
```

When not in interactive mode, the underscore character has
no special meaning.

2.8 Object Oriented Programming

So far, we've been used Python in a *procedural* way. *Procedural
programming* is a paradigm based on procedure (or function)
calls. *Procedural programming* is a form of *Imperative
programming*, which consists of using statements to change
the state of a program. It's just about describing *how* the
program should operate, by specifying a series of commands
to be executed.

On the other hand, Object Oriented Programming (OOP) is
based on idea of the interaction between "objects", which
have both a *state* and *behavior*. The state of an object is
represented in terms of *fields* (also referred to as *properties* or
attributes) and its behavior in terms of functions, commonly
referred to as *methods*, in the OOP context.

2.8.1 Classes and Objects

Allow me to start with practical examples and the theory will
follow.

We are going to create a class that represents dogs, which
will have attributes such as name and color. This class will also
define a possible behavior of dogs from this class, which is to
bark. Because they are special dogs, whenever they bark they
say their names:

```
class Dog:
    name = "Bobby"
```

```
    def bark(self):
        return self.name

snoopy = Dog()
lassie = Dog()
print(snoopy.bark())
print(lassie.bark())
```

(file classes1.py)

```
→ ~/StartCareerPython python classes1.py
Bobby
Bobby
```

Now let me explain this code.

The *class* definition works just like a function definition: before it can be put in effect, it must be executed.

A *class* definition has its own local namespace as well. The *class* Dog defines an *attribute* called **name** and a *method* called **bark**. Whenever you treat the class as a function, Dog(), you are actually creating a new *instance* of that class. Both snoopy and lassie are now two objects of type *Dog* and they are said to be instances of the class Dog.

The class definition is actually defining a new data type, which is *Dog*, just the same way *list* or *str* are data types in Python. The name self refers to the current instance being used. So when you invoke **snoopy.bark()**, self yields a reference to the snoopy object and **self.name** is accessing the attribute name of the object snoopy.

The downside of this code is that any dog we create will have the same name: Bobby. But we can take care of that by defining a method **__init__**. Whenever this method is defined in a class, the class instantiation will invoke it. This is quite useful to customize object creation with specific parameters.

Let's see how this works:

```
class Dog:
    def __init__(self, name):
        self.name = name

    def bark(self):
        return self.name

snoop = Dog("Snoopy")
lass = Dog("Lassie")
print(snoop.bark())
print(lass.bark())
```

(file classes1.py)

```
→ ~/StartCareerPython python classes1.py
Snoopy
Lassie
```

Much better, right? Well, actually the **bark** method is not doing much, because we can access the `name` of the dog without calling the method:

```
print(snoop.name)
print(lass.name)
```

This is called *attribute referencing* and you can do the same with the methods without using the parentheses, but what you will get is the *function object*.

You may be wondering why does the **bark** method take an argument (`self`) and we invoke it without passing any. This has got to do with how method invokations work in Python. The method call **snoop.bark()** is semantically equivalent to **Dog.bark(snoop)**. The same would go for a method with more arguments.

2.8.1.1 Class and Instance Variables

In the first example, before we defined the **__init__** method, `name` was what's called a *class variable*.

Class variables are shared amongst all the instances of that class, which means that they will all see the same value. Nonetheless, shared data has unexpected effects, depending on whether the attribute is of immutable or mutable data type.

Let's see what happens when an object tries to assign a new immutable object to a class variable:

```
class Dog:
    color = "brown"

    def __init__(self, name):
        self.name = name

    def bark(self):
        return self.name

snoop = Dog("Snoopy")
lass = Dog("Lassie")
print(snoop.color)
print(lass.color)
lass.color = "yellow"
print(snoop.color)
print(lass.color)
```
(file classes2.py)

```
➔ ~/StartCareerPython python classes2.py
brown
brown
brown
yellow
```

This shouldn't be surprising. `lass` and `snoop`'s color attribute at first reference the same object, but then `lass`'s color attribute points to a different one. If you print both attributes' **id** before and after you will see that their unique identifier changes (for `lass`, not for `snoop`).

If you wanted to change the value of `color` and still share it amongst all the instances of that class, you should do `Dog.color = <new-value>` instead.

But what if the class variable is of a mutable type? Let's see what happens:

```python
class Dog:
    siblings = []

    def __init__(self, name):
        self.name = name

    def bark(self):
        return self.name

    def add_sibling(self, sib):
        self.siblings.append(sib)

snoop = Dog("Snoopy")
lass = Dog("Lassie")
print(snoop.siblings)
lass.add_sibling(Dog("Max"))
print(snoop.siblings[0].name)
```

(file classes3.py)

```
➜ ~/StartCareerPython python classes3.py
[]
Max
```

The list would be shared by all `Dog` instances. Try printing `Dog.siblings[0].name` afterwards to see the result.

If you want to use and change values of class variables, always make sure to use the notation `MyClass.variable`, like **Dog.siblings.append(Dog("Max"))** .

But to use instance variables, you must design your class properly. Let's say that you wanted `siblings` to be an instance variable instead. This is how you should do it:

```python
class Dog:
    def __init__(self, name):
        self.name = name
        self.siblings = []  # empty list for each Dog

    def bark(self):
```

```
        return self.name

    def add_sibling(self, sib):
        self.siblings.append(sib)

snoop = Dog("Snoopy")
lass = Dog("Lassie")
print(snoop.siblings)
lass.add_sibling(Dog("Max"))
print(snoop.siblings)
print(lass.siblings)
```

(file classes3.py)

```
➜  ~/StartCareerPython python classes3.py
[]
[]
[<__main__.Dog object at 0x10be36240>]
```

2.8.1.2 A note on `self`

In Python, the word `self` doesn't have any special meaning, it's purely a convention. Nonetheless, such conventions exist to promote code readability. Also, probably most of the IDEs and editors follow this convention and will immediately highlight the word `self`.

Other languages, like Java, use the `this` keyword, which is actually a reserved word of the language.

2.8.2 Encapsulation

Encapsulation is a technique used in OOP for information hiding.

For example, if you want to disable direct access to the attributes of an object from your code and force it to be done through methods. In order words: you design your class in such a way that its attributes are only accessible through methods.

Languages like Java, PHP or C++ have keywords, that are used alongside with methods and attributes definitions when defining a class, to limit the access: *private*, *protected* or *public*.

Encapsulation is a powerful abstraction that facilitates *code refactoring*, for example. If you design a class that exposes methods to be used publicly and you want to change how your class represents its internal data, you can enforce this internal data to be accessed only by those public methods, **as long as you don't change the way the methods are called**.

Unfortunately, Python doesn't benefit from such constructs and encapsulation is done in a more limited way via a mechanism called *name mangling*.

Note: you will often come across the acronym **API**, which means *Application Program Interface*. An API is basically a set of routines and protocols for building software applications. When you create your own classes to build your software (or facilitate the development of external software), they will be exposing a public API, which will be all the methods and attributes publicly available, as well as protocols that define how they should be used. The same goes for function definitions in modules that you create and can be imported somewhere else.

In the context of a class definition, any name starting with two or more underscores and ending with at most one underscore will be subject to *name mangling*.

This means that if a class `MyClass` has an attribute `__name`, it will be textually replaced by `_MyClass__name`. Let's see how this works:

```python
class Dog:
    def __init__(self, name):
        self.__name = name

    def bark(self):
        return self.__name

snoop = Dog("Snoopy")
print(snoop.__name)
```
(file classes4.py)

```
→ ~/StartCareerPython python classes4.py
Traceback (most recent call last):
```

```
File "classes4.py", line 9, in <module>
    print(snoop.__name)
AttributeError: 'Dog' object has no attribute '__name'
```

The attribute `__name` cannot be accessed directly. You would have to call **bark** to retrieve its value or implement a method to change it. The reason why this happens is because it was textually replaced with `_Dog__name`:

```
print(snoop._Dog__name)
```
(file classes4.py modified)

```
➜  ~/StartCareerPython python classes4.py
Snoopy
```

Let's design our `Dog` class in a different way in order to use a private attribute via *name mangling*:

```
class Dog:
    def __init__(self, name):
        self.__name = name

    def get_name(self):
        return self.__name

    def set_name(self, new_name):
        self.__name = new_name

snoop = Dog("Snoopy")
print(snoop.get_name())
snoop.set_name("Max")
print(snoop.get_name())
```
(file classes5.py)

```
➜  ~/StartCareerPython python classes5.py
Snoopy
Max
```

However, this approach is not considered *Pythonic* (doesn't follow the good practices in Python).

Programs written in Java, for example, make extensive use of *getters* and *setters* for attributes, meaning that in general the attributes are private and the classes have methods for retrieving and changing their values. In Python, this is not considered a good practice. Instead, it's preferable to use *properties*, which are a special construct in Python (not to be mixed with the alternative name to attributes in OOP).

2.8.2.1 Properties vs Getters and Setters

Like I mentioned, in languages like Java it is very common to have the attributes in a class private and a bunch of getters and setters (methods that get and set values of properties).

If you are just setting or getting a value directly, you might think that there isn't much use to it (and many people agree with you).

```
# The getters and setters way
object.set_number(42)
print(object.get_number())

# The direct access way
object.number = 42
print(object.number)
```

So why would you have extra functions when you can just access the attributes directly? This is time spent writing extra code, time spent understanding extra code and makes your code bigger.

Nonetheless, if you know the value of an attribute depends on some complex formula, it makes more sense to just write that formula in one single place instead of writing it everywhere you want to set the value, right? Because if later you want to change that formula, you would need to search, in your code, for all the spots where you are setting the value and change the formula, thus spending lots of time...and being more prone to making mistakes.

This is where setters and getters are useful: when setting a value is more than a simple assignment (or if getting is also not straightforward).

In Python, you achieve this with **properties**.

A property is actually a class in Python, but in general they are used as *decorators*. In short, a *decorator* is a function that applies a transformation to another function, but is applied using the @Wrapper syntax. In fact, the decorator mechanism in Python (and in other language) is an implementation of the Decorator *design pattern* (more about design patterns in section *2.8.4 Design Patterns*).

A decorator allows behavior to be added to objects dynamically (or statically), without affecting other objects of the same class. This may start being a bit confusing, so let me give you an example so that it starts making sense. Bear with me!

```python
class Dog:
    def __init__(self, name):
        self.__name = name


    @property
    def name(self):
        return self.__name


    @name.setter
    def name(self, new_name):
        self.__name = new_name

snoop = Dog("Snoopy")
print(snoop.name)
snoop.name = "Max"
print(snoop.name)
```
(file decorators.py)

```
→ ~/StartCareerPython python decorators.py
Snoopy
Max
```

The @ before `property` turns the **name** method into a getter for __name.

Internally, a decorator is actually a function that returns another function, using the @`wrapper` syntax. It "decorates" a function with certain features. The two following approaches are equivalent, semantically speaking:

```
# With @wrapper syntax
@property
def name(self):
    ...

# With regular function syntax
def name(self):
    ...
name = property(name)
```

You can read more about the property class in the *official documentation*[22].

2.8.3 Inheritance and Composition

Composition means that objects can contain other objects in their instance variables. Let's see a quick and simple example:

```
class Dog:
    def __init__(self, name):
        self.__name = name
        self.siblings = []


    @property
    def name(self):
        return self.__name
```

```
    @name.setter
    def name(self, new_name):
        self.__name = new_name

snoop = Dog("Snoop")
snoop.siblings.append(Dog("Max"))
snoop.siblings.append(Dog("Lassie"))
print([d.name for d in snoop.siblings])
```

(file classes6.py)

```
→ ~/StartCareerPython python classes6.py
['Max', 'Lassie']
```

In this case, objects of the class `Dog` may contain other objects in their instance variable `siblings`.

Inheritance, on the other hand, allows you to arrange your classes in a hierarchy and is quite useful for code reusability.

Let's say that now you want to create another class, `Cat`, which shares some attributes with `Dog`, for example `name` and `color`. We want the objects of the class `Cat` to **meow** and the objects of class `Dog` to **bark**. This time we won't make these attributes private, just for the sake of simplicity.

These are our classes without using inheritance:

```
class Dog:
    def __init__(self, name, color):
        self.name = name
        self.color = color

    def bark(self):
        print("My name is {} and I'm {}".format(
            self.name, self.color)
        )

class Cat:
    def __init__(self, name, color):
        self.name = name
        self.color = color
```

```
    def meow(self):
        print("My name is {} and I'm{}".format(
            self.name, self.color)
        )

snoop = Dog("Snoopy", "black")
garf = Cat("Garfield", "orange")
snoop.bark()
garf.meow()
```

(file classes7.py)

```
→ ~/StartCareerPython python classes7.py
My name is Snoopy and I'm black
My name is Garfield and I'm orange
```

Basically, most of the code was duplicated and this is one the things we want to avoid. If you think in terms of the real life scenario, both dogs and cats are animals.

Let's say that all animals have at least two properties in common: *name* and *color*. What we can do is create a class `Animal`, which will be the *base class* or *superclass*, and have `Dog` and `Cat` *inherit* from it. These two will be the *subclasses* or *derived classes*.

```
class Animal:
    def __init__(self, name, color):
        self.name = name
        self.color = color

class Dog(Animal):
    def bark(self):
        print("My name is {} and I'm {}".format(
            self.name, self.color)
        )

class Cat(Animal):
    def meow(self):
        print("My name is {} and I'm {}".format(
            self.name, self.color)
        )

snoop = Dog("Snoopy", "black")
garf = Cat("Garfield", "orange")
```

```
snoop.bark()
garf.meow()
```

(file classes8.py)

```
→ ~/StartCareerPython python classes8.py
My name is Snoopy and I'm black
My name is Garfield and I'm orange
```

Much better, but we still have duplicate code, even though
the methods **bark** and **meow** have different names.

We don't really need to have methods with different names,
as long as the new common method translates the action.
What if we have one single method **speak** for both classes?
That will even give us much more flexibility.

Let me show you how:

```
class Animal:
    def __init__(self, name, color):
        self.name = name
        self.color = color

    def speak(self):
        print("My name is {} and I'm {}".format(
            self.name, self.color)
        )

class Dog(Animal):
    pass

class Cat(Animal):
    pass

animals = []
animals.append(Dog("Snoop", "black"))
animals.append(Dog("Max", "white"))
animals.append(Cat("Fluffy", "yellow"))
animals.append(Dog("Lassie", "brown"))

for animal in animals:
    animal.speak()
```

(file classes8.py modified)

```
→ ~/StartCareerPython python classes8.py
My name is Snoop and I'm black
My name is Max and I'm white
My name is Fluffy and I'm yellow
My name is Lassie and I'm brown
```

The `pass` statement is just a *null* operation, meaning that when executed nothing really happens. It is a great placeholder for when no code needs to be executed and yet a statement is required.

In the `for` loop, we don't really care what kind of animal the iterator is returning, because we know that both cats and dogs share a *common interface* through their base class `Animal`.

In OOP this is called *polymorphism*, and it refers to when calling code can be completely agnostic to which class an object belongs to. If we had another subclass of `Animal`, let's say `Bird`, we could still invoke the method **speak** without a problem.

Note that instances of `Cat` and `Dog` classes are also instances of `Animal`:

```
snoop = Dog("Snoop", "black")
print(isinstance(snoop, Dog))
print(isinstance(snoop, Animal))
```

```
→ ~/StartCareerPython python classes8.py
True
True
```

Instances of a class are instances of all the parents of that class and parents of the parents.

2.8.3.1 Abstract Classes
Our code above allows us to create instances of `Animal`, which might not be ideal.

In OOP, there is something called *abstract class*, which is a class that cannot be instantiated directly. It may not even provide any implementation, only methods headers. Methods without any implementation are called *abstract methods*. This is a useful mechanism to define a common interface for derived classes, without being worried with the underlying implementation.

Languages like Java or PHP also provide *Interfaces*. In Python, we may benefit from these constructs via the `abc` module and a few decorators.

Let's turn our `Animal` class into an *abstract class*.

```
from abc import ABCMeta, abstractmethod

class Animal(metaclass=ABCMeta):
    def __init__(self, name, color):
        self.name = name
        self.color = color


    @abstractmethod
    def speak(self):
        pass
```

(file classes9.py)

```
>>> import classes9
>>> animal = classes9.Animal("Snoopy", "black")
Traceback (most recent call last):
 File "<stdin>", line 1, in <module>
TypeError: Can't instantiate abstract class Animal with
abstract methods speak
```

In Python, when using the module `abc`, a class is said to be *abstract* if it indicates that its *metaclass* is `ABCMeta` and if it has at least one *abstract method*. In our situation, the class `Animal` has `ABCMeta` as *metaclass* and it has one *abstract method*: **speak**. Don't worry about what a *metaclass* is for now.

Unlike what OOP theory dictates, abstract methods in Python can have an implementation.

Let's change our method **speak** and add `Dog` as a subclass of `Animal`:

```python
from abc import ABCMeta, abstractmethod

class Animal(metaclass=ABCMeta):
    def __init__(self, name, color):
        self.name = name
        self.color = color


    @abstractmethod
    def speak(self):
        print("My name is {} and I'm {}".format(
          self.name, self.color)
        )

class Dog(Animal):
    def speak(self):
        super().speak()
```

(file classes9.py modified)

And we have to reload our module, because its contents changed. You can either re-start the interactive shell or use **reload** from `importlib`:

```python
>>> import importlib
>>> importlib.reload(classes9)
<module 'classes9' from
'/Users/pmpro/StartCareerPython/classes9.py'>
```

And now we can instantiate Dog:

```python
>>> d = classes9.Dog("Snoopy", "black")
>>> d.speak()
My name is Snoopy and I'm black
```

We were only able to instantiate `Dog` because in its definition the method **speak** is overridden. If it wasn't, we wouldn't be able.

Try to remove the definition of **speak** from the Dog class and try to instantiate it. The method speak in Dog is using the built-in **super**. This is a way of delegating method calls to parent class. In our situation, we are invoking the method **speak** from the parent class Animal. In fact, we can add code after the **super** call:

```
class Dog(Animal):
    def speak(self):
        super().speak()
        print("Say something else")
```
(file classes9.py modified)

```
>>> importlib.reload(classes9)
>>> d = classes9.Dog("Snoopy", "black")
>>> d.speak()
My name is Snoopy and I'm black
Say something else
```

Note that super().speak() does the same as super(Dog, self).speak(). More information about **super** can be found in the *official documentation*[23].

2.8.3.2 Multiple Inheritance
Python also supports another feature from OOP, which is *multiple inheritance*. As the name suggests, a class can have more than one base class:

```
class MyClass(Base1, Base2):
    pass
```

Inherited attributes or methods are searched left-to-right. First, MyClass is searched. If the attribute or method is not found, then it will be searched in Base1 and, then, recursively in all its base classes. If it's not found, then the same procedure takes place for Base2 and so on.

```python
from abc import ABCMeta, abstractmethod

class Animal(metaclass=ABCMeta):
    def __init__(self, name, color):
        self.name = name
        self.color = color


    @abstractmethod
    def speak(self):
        print("My name is {} and I'm {}".format(
            self.name, self.color)
        )

class Pet:
    def cuddle(self):
        print("Just cuddling.")

class Dog(Animal, Pet):
    def speak(self):
        super().speak()

d = Dog("Snoopy", "black")
d.speak()
d.cuddle()
```

(file classes10.py)

```
→ ~/StartCareerPython python classes10.py
My name is Snoopy and I'm black
Just cuddling.
```

2.8.4 Design Patterns

Design patterns are general repeatable solutions for problems that occur frequently in software development. They are a generic recipe that can be applied to a myriad of situations.

Design patterns vary in the nature of problems they are supposed to solve. For example, *decorator* is a *structural pattern*. Iterators are an implementation of the behavioral design pattern *Iterator*.

Even though it's outside the scope of this book to discuss in depth *Design Patterns* (I would probably need a separate book just for that), it's still something that I must mention and, hopefully, spark some curiosity. Knowledge and experience with *Design Patterns* is something that you should aim for, as it will improve your problem solving and software design skills. One of the most important references in this topic is the book *Design Patterns: Elements of Reusable Object Oriented Software*[24]. The authors of the book are usually referred to as the *Gang of Four*.

2.8.5 Notes on Classes

Like functions, classes are a *callable* data type, meaning that you can apply the *call* expression on them (with opening and closing parentheses).

Whenever a class is *called*, its __new__ method is invoked, in order to create an instance of that class. If the class definition also includes the method __init__, then it will be called immediately after __new__, but before the instance of the class is returned. The method __init__, as we've seen, customizes the newly created instance.

Classes recognize special methods whose names follow a certain pattern. By defining or overriding those methods, you can customize the behavior of a class. The special methods follow the pattern __*__. As such, it's not advisable for you to name attributes or methods in your class following this pattern, because there may be a chance that they will be a system-defined name in future versions of Python.

I won't cover all the special methods that you can (re)define, but this is something to take into consideration when you want to take *the next step*. You can find explanations about them in the section *Special Method Names*[25] of *Python Language Reference*.

Another aspect to take into consideration is the concept of *static methods* and *class methods*.
Let's compare these two types of methods with instance methods:

```python
class A:
    def foo(self, bar):
        print(bar)

    @classmethod
    def foo_class(cls, bar):
        print(cls)
        print(bar)

    @staticmethod
    def foo_static(bar):
        print(bar)

a = A()
a.foo("Hello")
a.foo_class("Hello")
a.foo_static("Hello")
```
(file classes11.py)

```
➔ ~/StartCareerPython python classes11.py
Hello
<class '__main__.A'>
Hello
Hello
```

foo is an *instance method*, and a is implicitly passed to **foo** when it's invoked. **a.foo("Hello")** is semantically equivalent to **A.foo(a, "Hello")**.

On the other hand, **foo_class** is a *class method*. You can either call it using an object or a class name, like **A.foo_class("Hello")**. When you call it using an object, the class of the object is implicitly passed to the method. If you call it using a class, that class will be passed to the method. **foo** is aware of the object and **foo_class** is aware of the class.

Finally, **foo_static** is unaware of both the object and the class. As a matter of fact, static methods in Python exist mostly for stylistic and organizational purposes. This means that if a function belongs logically to a class but doesn't need to be aware of it, you can place it as a static method for that class. This is a way of preventing module namespace pollution.

Our static method can be called either via object or via class name: **a.foo_static("Hello")** and **A.foo_static("Hello")** are semantically equivalent.

2.9 Functional Programming

This section is not intended to cover exhaustively what Functional Programming is. Nonetheless, I will speak briefly about it, give you the necessary insights and then delve immediately into the features that Python provides to program in a functional style.

Functional programming is a style (or a paradigm) of writing computer programs where computations are treated as evaluation of mathematical functions on one hand, and on the other hand avoids side effects and mutable data. Here are some of the key principles behind functional programming:

HIGHER-ORDER AND FIRST-CLASS FUNCTIONS
In functional style, functions are said to be higher-order, which means that they can take other functions as arguments and also return functions as values. On the other hand, they are also first-class citizens, which means that they can appear anywhere in a program, where other first-class types (like integers) would.

Pure functions have no side effects, meaning that for the same input you will always get the same output. This differs a lot from OOP, for example, where objects maintain state and method calls may not only be affected by that state but will also change it. Thus, pure functions are easier to test due to their predictability. Also, if there is no data dependency between two pure functions, you can reverse the order by which they are executed or even execute them in parallel.

RECURSION

Often, looping (or iteration) in functional languages is accomplished via recursion. As explained before, recursive functions call themselves until the base case is reached.

NO SIDE EFFECTS

Also known as referential transparency, having no side effects is a property of purely functional languages. This means that there are no assignment statements, because the value of a variable doesn't change once it was defined.

Python is multi-paradigm, because it has features and constructs for procedural, object oriented and functional programming paradigms. Also, Python programs written in functional style don't completely follow a pure functional approach, because functions have local assignment of variables.

Let's now see some of the features that Python offers so that you can mix a functional style of programming with procedural and/or object oriented.

2.9.1 The `lambda` expression

The `lambda` expression allows us to create anonymous functions, which are functions that don't have a name. Just like regular functions, they have a parameter list, but they are a bit more limited in their capabilities. For instance, you cannot have a `return` statement or even a regular `if-else` statement.

Let's check a few examples:

```
>>> add_numbers = lambda x, y: x+y
>>> add_numbers(3, 4)
7
```

`lambda arguments: expression` actually *yields* a function object.

```
>>> type(add_numbers)
<class 'function'>
```

The value returned by the function object yielded is the result of evaluating the expression. Let's see another example:

```
>>> add = lambda x, y: x+y if x > y else x+y**2
>>> add(3, 4)
19
>>> add(4, 3)
7
```

The expression basically means "evaluate x+y if x is greater than y or evaluate x+y**2 otherwise".

It is semantically equivalent to the following named function:

```
>>> def add(x, y):
...     if x > y:
```

```
...            return x+y
...      else:
...            return x+y**2
```

So if we can achieve the same (and more) with regular named functions, why would we use lambda expressions?

Well, functions are in general defined to wrap behavior that is required in several parts of the code, thus avoiding code duplication. They promote code reusability, readability and modularity. But there are situations when you don't want to define a function because a behavior will be required only once, and a lambda makes more sense, especially if it's quite simple.

We'll see usage of lambdas in the next sections, so that you can be convinced.

Note: the scoping and namespace rules in lambdas are the same applied to regular functions.

Let's see an example where a certain behavior is manifested as expected and yet many programmers fail to predict it. (this example can be found in the **FAQ**[26] of the official documentation)

```
>>> squares = []
>>> for x in range(5):
...      squares.append(lambda: x**2)
```

This code is creating a list with 5 elements, where each element is a function object. The idea is that the function object returns an integer which is the square of the index of the function object in the list. So you would expect the call squares[1]() to return 1, squares[2]() to return 4 and so forth. Let's see what happens:

```
>>> squares[1]()
16
>>> squares[2]()
16
```

How is this possible? The problem is that x is not a local name to the lambdas: it is a name in the outer scope created by the for loop. This name is accessed when the functions are called, not when they are defined:

```
>>> x = 3
>>> def print_x():
```

```
...        print(x)
...
>>> print_x()
3
>>> x = 4
>>> print_x()
4
```

When the `for` loop finishes, the value of `x` is 4, which means that every function call will return `4**2`. To solve this problem and print what you want, you must create a name that is local to each function, by using a *default* value:

```
>>> squares = []
>>> for x in range(5):
...        squares.append(lambda n=x: n**2)
...
>>> squares[1]()
1
>>> squares[3]()
9
```

2.9.2 Iterators revisited with Generators

Iterators are probably one of the most important features that Python offers to allow you build programs in a functional style.

By now, you already know what iterators are and some use cases. You also know their relationship with *iterable* objects (and, hopefully, remember that they are not the same). Iterators are returned when you pass an *iterable* to a `for` loop, for example. You can also retrieve an iterator from an *iterable* by passing the *iterable* directly to the **iter** built-in function:

```
>>> it = iter(["a", "b", "c"])
>>> it
<list_iterator object at 0x1021b14a8>
>>> it.__next__()
'a'
>>> next(it)
'b'
>>> it.__next__()
'c'
>>> next(it)
```

```
Traceback (most recent call last):
  File "<stdin>", line 1, in <module>
StopIteration
```

Note that calling the method __next__ from the iterator object is exactly the same as passing the iterator to the built-in function **next**.

As we've seen, lots of data types support iterators, such as sequence types (lists, tuples, strings, etc), file objects, etc. What if we want to create our own iterators?

Let's see an example with a class that represents a shopping list and contains a list with items as an attribute:

```
class Item:
    def __init__(self, name, price):
        self.name = name
        self.price = price

    def __str__(self):
        return "{}({})".format(self.name, self.price)

class ShoppingList:
    def __init__(self):
        self.items = []

    def __iter__(self):
        return iter(self.items)

groceries = ShoppingList()
groceries.items.append(Item("Cucumber", 0.99))
groceries.items.append(Item("Bananas", 1.7))
groceries.items.append(Item("Strawberries", 3.4))

for item in groceries:
    print(item)
```

(file functional1.py)

Two things to pay attention in this code:

- The class Item defines the method __str__. If you recall what I've told you before, overriding special methods allows you to customize the behavior of a class. If you override __str__ you will be able to define the string representation of an object of that class, which means that you can print it in a nicer way.

- The class `ShoppingList` defines the method **__iter__**, which is also a special method that is invoked whenever you pass an instance of this class to a `for` statement and returns an iterator for that object. For now, the **__iter__** method is returning the default iterator of a list object using the built-in function **iter**, but we can also customize our iterator.

```
→ ~/StartCareerPython python functional1.py
Cucumber(0.99)
Bananas(1.7)
Strawberries(3.4)
```

Now let's suppose that we want to print only the items whose price is less than or equal to `2.0`. You wouldn't have any difficulty in achieving this with a `for` loop and an `if` statement, right?

```
for item in groceries:
    if item.price <= 2.0:
        print(item)
```

But the problem is that this `for` loop is doing two things: on one hand, it's filtering the items returned by the iterator and on the other hand is printing the filtered items.

What if we had an iterator that returns the filtered items?

Well, we could, of course, define a class called `ShoppingListIterator` (for example) and define the methods **__iter__** and **__next__** in that class (to be conformant with the *Iterator Protocol*). Then the **__iter__** method in `ShoppingList` class would return an instance of `ShoppingListIterator`. The **__next__** method would return the next item (and decide how to return it) and raise

`StopIteration` as soon as no more items existed to be returned.

It's a lot of code just for something so "simple". Fortunately, Python provides the `yield` statement which gives you the ability of creating generators in a few lines of code. You also have *generator expressions* which are very similar to *list comprehensions*.

Let's explore both ways of creating generators that generate iterators!

2.9.2.1 The `yield` statement

Generators are a special class of functions that have the ability to resume their computation when they are called over and over.

A normal function, as we've seen so far, computes a value and returns it (or implicitly returns `None`). It has a local namespace that is created when you call the function and destroyed when the function returns.

A generator, in turn, won't destroy the local variables when the function exits. A generator has the ability to resume its execution from the point where it exited the last time.

A generator is a function that has a `yield` statement (actually you can only use the yield statement in the body of a function) and, like `return`, it returns the value it's *yielding*. The difference is that the execution is suspended when the `yield` statement is reached, and when the `return` statement is reached the execution is terminated.

Here's a very simple example of a generator that returns an iterator:

```
def good_morning_gen():
    yield "Good"
    yield "Morning"

gen = good_morning_gen()
print(gen)
print(next(gen))
```

```
print(next(gen))
print(next(gen))
```

(file functional2.py)

```
→ ~/StartCareerPython python functional2.py
<generator object good_morning_gen at 0x10eb38830>
Good
Morning
Traceback (most recent call last):
 File "functional2.py", line 9, in <module>
   print(next(gen))
StopIteration
```

In a generator function, the execution is stopped when the bottom of its body or a `return` statement is reached and no more values can be yielded. Here's yet another generator function that this time returns all the items in our shopping list that are priced at `2.0` or less:

```python
class Item:
    def __init__(self, name, price):
        self.name = name
        self.price = price

    def __str__(self):
        return "{}({})".format(self.name, self.price)

class ShoppingList:
    def __init__(self):
        self.items = []

    def __iter__(self):
        for item in self.items:
            if item.price <= 2.0:
                yield item

groceries = ShoppingList()
groceries.items.append(Item("Cucumber", 0.99))
groceries.items.append(Item("Bananas", 1.7))
groceries.items.append(Item("Strawberries", 3.4))

for item in groceries:
    print(item)
```

(file functional3.py)

```
→ ~/StartCareerPython python functional3.py
Cucumber(0.99)
Bananas(1.7)
```

The objective is to illustrate how simple and yet powerful the generators are. Nonetheless, for this situation you'd be better off using the built-in function **filter**.

```python
class Item:
    def __init__(self, name, price):
        self.name = name
        self.price = price

    def __str__(self):
        return "{}({})".format(self.name, self.price)

class ShoppingList:
    def __init__(self):
        self.items = []

    def __iter__(self):
        return iter(self.items)

groceries = ShoppingList()
groceries.items.append(Item("Cucumber", 0.99))
groceries.items.append(Item("Bananas", 1.7))
groceries.items.append(Item("Strawberries", 3.4))

for item in filter(lambda i: i.price <= 2.0, groceries):
    print(item)
```

(file functional4.py)

```
→ ~/StartCareerPython python functional4.py
Cucumber(0.99)
Bananas(1.7)
```

I'll leave it as exercise for you to try to figure out on your own what is that code doing. Don't worry, I will explain it later in section *2.9.3 map and filter*.

Let's see another example of generators. Let's suppose that we have a text file with a bunch of lines. Some lines start with the character # and others don't. We want to do something only to the lines that don't start with #. In this simple example, we just want to print such lines.

Here's one first solution without using generators:

```
with open("functional5.txt") as f:
    for line in f:
        line = line.strip()
        if not line.startswith("#"):
            print(line)
```

Here are the contents of *functional5.txt*:

```
# This line is not valid
This is the first valid line.
And this is the second valid line.
# Another invalid line
# And yet another
We're back to valid lines
And this is the last valid line
# And the last invalid line
```

And the result of the execution:

```
➜ ~/StartCareerPython python functional5.py
This is the first valid line.
And this is the second valid line.
We're back to valid lines
And this is the last valid line
```

Again, the `for` loop is doing more than one thing. In fact, it's doing 3 things: it strips the current line, it checks whether the line is valid or not and then it does something with the line. There is not exactly separation of concerns. Let's see how we can achieve this with a generator:

```
def valid_lines(lines):
    for line in lines:
        line = line.strip()
```

```
        if not line.startswith("#"):
            yield line

with open("functional5.txt") as f:
    for line in valid_lines(f):
        print(line)
```

(file functional5.py)

```
→ ~/StartCareerPython python functional5.py
This is the first valid line.
And this is the second valid line.
We're back to valid lines
And this is the last valid line
```

This code is much better for several reasons. First of all, the body of the `for` loop is just concerned about what to do with valid lines.

Secondly, the generator **valid_lines** takes as argument any *iterable* that produces strings, not just file objects. This means that it is extremely easy to test, because you can just provide a list of strings and make sure it works fine.

And finally, you can very easily customize your generator in order to use other criteria to determine whether a line is valid or not.

Let's make the necessary changes and also start adding some comments to the code:

```
def valid_lines(lines, is_valid):
    """
    Generator function that creates an iterator that
    returns valid lines.

    :param lines: Any iterable that returns strings
    :param is_valid: A function object that takes a
                     string as argument and returns a
                     boolean value
    """
    for line in lines:
        line = line.strip()
        if is_valid(line):
            yield line
```

```
with open("functional5.txt") as f:
    for line in valid_lines(f,
        lambda x: not x.startswith("#")):
        print(line)
```
(file functional6.py)

Much better! We have now a generator that is fully customizable in the way it creates an iterator that returns the next item. And it's pretty easy to test.

2.9.2.2 Generator expression

So far, we've seen how to create generators using the `yield` statement. You can also create generators using a generator expression ("genexp"), which is similar to a list comprehension in almost every way, except for the fact that it uses parentheses instead of square brackets.

```
>>> lines = ["# This line is not valid\n", "This is the
↵first valid line.\n", "# Another invalid line\n"]
>>> valid_lines = (line.strip() for line in lines if
↵not line.startswith("#"))
>>> valid_lines
<generator object <genexpr> at 0x10fcf8a40>
>>> for line in valid_lines:
...     print(line)
...
This is the first valid line.
```

`valid_lines` is a generator object and creates an iterator. Now one may think "Why can't I use a list comprehension instead? Why do I need a generator?".

Well, you can use a list comprehension and build the entire list and iterate over that list. But this also means that if the list is huge, you would have to build the entire list beforehand. This is one of the reasons why generators are so attractive, due to a property called *lazy evaluation*.

Lazy evaluation refers to the fact that the entire range of values is not built beforehand (and potentially exhausting memory). Instead, values are computed on demand, as they are needed, but unlike lists you cannot refer to values by indexing them.

2.9.3 `map` and `filter`

Python has plenty of built-in functions and modules that allow you to program in a functional style. Two of the most used functions are **map** and **filter**, and in some way they duplicate the features of generators expressions.

The **map** function takes as arguments a function `f` and *iterables* iterA, iterB, etc. It then returns an iterator where each element is the result of calling the function f with the current elements of each iterable: `f(iterA[0], iterB[0], …)`, `f(iterA[1], iterB[1], …)`, and so on. The iterator stops when the smallest *iterable* is exhausted. This also means that the function `f` must expect as many arguments as the number of *iterables* you pass to the function **map**.

Let's see a simple example:

```
>>> words = ["Hello", "world", "gOod", "mORNING"]
>>> list(map(str.upper, words))
['HELLO', 'WORLD', 'GOOD', 'MORNING']
```

In this simple example, the map function applies **str.upper** method to each of the strings in the list `words`. Let's see another example:

```
>>> list(map(lambda x: x*2, words))
['HelloHello', 'worldworld', 'gOodgOod',
'mORNINGmORNING']
```

And now an example with 2 *iterables*:

```
>>> names = ["John", "Mary", "Bob", "Peter"]
>>> list(map(lambda x, y: x+y, words, names))
['HelloJohn', 'worldMary', 'gOodBob', 'mORNINGPeter']
```

The **filter** function, on the other hand, returns an iterator over the elements of an *iterable* that meet the condition defined by a function, which means that it takes a function and an *iterable* as arguments. The function returns a boolean and the iterator only returns elements from the *iterable* that make the function return `True`.

Let's see how it works:

```
>>> words
['Hello', 'world', 'gOod', 'mORNING']
>>> list(filter(lambda x: len(x) < 5, words))
['gOod']
```

Again, the function that **filter** takes as argument is going to be applied to each of the elements of the *iterable*. Only those elements that make the function return `True` will be returned by the iterator created by **filter**.

Like I said, **map** and **filter** kind of duplicate the features of generator expressions. Which means that some of the examples above where I explained generators could have been solved with **map** and **filter**.

Recall, for instance, the example in *functional6.py*, where we receive a text file as an input (which a bunch of lines, some starting with #) and iterate over the lines and only do some stuff if the line is valid.

Here is a way to solve it using map and filter:

```
with open("functional5.txt") as f:
    for line in map(lambda l: l.strip(),
```

```
        filter(lambda x: not x.startswith("#"), f)):
    print(line)
```
(file functional7.py)

Even though this code is much shorter, which one is more readable? Remember that when you write software, you are doing it for a computer, for yourself and for the person who will maintain / extend / fix it.

Programmers' time is more precious that computers' time, in most of the cases. Nonetheless, a good rule of thumb when writing one-liners is to write it in such a way that reading it out loud still makes sense. In this case, "in the `for` loop we are iterating over lines in a text file, stripping and printing them, as long as they that don't start with a # character".

Challenge: give two lists, one with countries and another with languages, build a dictionary where each key is a country and the respective value is its language. The keys must be in lowercase and must be at most 7 characters long.

```
>>> countries = ["Senegal", "Netherlands", "United
↵States", "England", "India"]
>>> languages = ["FR", "NL", "EN", "EN", "HI"]
>>> d
{'senegal': 'FR', 'england': 'EN', 'india': 'HI'}
```

In the code above, d is the resulting dictionary. Do so just by using **map**, **filter** and **dict**.

2.9.4 **any** and `all`

These two built-in function inspect the truth value of each element in an *iterable*. **any** will return `True` if any of the elements is `True` and **all** will return `True` if all the elements are `True`. Note that an empty sequence (empty list, empty string, etc) evaluates to `True` with **all** and `False` with **any**. Let's see a few examples:

```
>>> any([3 > 5, 0, False])
False
>>> any([3 > 5, 1, False])
True
>>> any([3 < 5, 0, False])
True
>>> all([2 < 4, 0 != 1, True])
True
>>> all([])
True
```

2.9.5 The `itertools` and `functools` modules

I am not covering these two modules, but I will still quickly
write about them and urge you to explore both when you have
the time, before you feel the need. `itertools` module
contains lots of iterators that you can use out of the box and
its functions fall in the following categories:

- Functions that create a new iterator based on an existing one.
- Functions for treating the elements of an iterator as function arguments.
- Functions for selecting portions of the output of an iterator.
- Functions for grouping the output of an iterator.

The `functools` module, on the other hand, contains
plenty of higher-order functions, the most useful being
functools.partial().

Make sure you read the *Functional Programming HOW-TO*[27]
in the official documentation, as well as the help of those two
modules in the interactive shell.

2.10 Testing your code

When your software grows in size and complexity, you will have several communicating parts inside your program. Values returned by certain functions will be used as input for others, or maybe something you retrieve from a database or from a file or the internet will be used as input for functions that will produce results for other functions and so on.

Because humans aren't perfect, more often than not the software will contain errors and produce undesirable results. When bugs are found, someone (usually the person that wrote the software) must fix them. Debugging and fixing bugs takes a great portion of time that could be used in a more productive way. This time spent by developers' costs companies a lot of money.

Many papers, books and articles mention percentages of time that software developers spend fixing bugs. Even though these numbers differ a bit from paper to paper, the truth is that they all agree on the fact that on average more than 50% of a developer's time is spent fixing bugs.

One way of mitigating this problem is to properly test the code you write. Even though many developers claim that properly testing code takes time, the truth is that this time should be seen as an investment. Not only it is less than the time you spend fixing bugs, but it's also a way of newcomers to understand your code.

One of the most common ways of testing your code is with *Unit Testing*. Unit Testing refers to testing units of code and these units may vary in type. For example, when developing using procedural or functional style, a unit of code is a module or a function, whereas in OOP the unit of code is a class or a method.

The basic building blocks of unit testing are called *Test Cases*, which are single scenarios with sets of conditions under which you will determine if your software or one of its features is working as expected. Ideally, the testing code of each Test Case instance should be self-contained, so that they can be run in isolation or in arbitrary order.

Now that you have a bit of background, let's see how this works in Python. We start by defining a couple of functions inside *my_module.py*:

```python
def add_numbers(x, y):
    if x > y:
        return x+y
    else:
        return x**2 + y**2

def func(x, y):
    if isinstance(x, int) and isinstance(y, int):
        return x+y
    else:
        raise TypeError("x and y must be integers")
```

(file my_module.py)

And now we will create our unit test in a file called, for example, *test_my_module.py*.

Python has a built-in module `unittest`, which provides lots of features and constructs for unit testing. For the majority of the users, just a subset of these features is more than enough, but you can do some advanced stuff as well if you want.

Let's see how we create our unit test:

```python
import unittest

import my_module

class TestMyModule(unittest.TestCase):
    def test_add_numbers(self):
        self.assertEqual(
            my_module.add_numbers(4, 3), 7
        )
        self.assertEqual(
```

```
            my_module.add_numbers(3, 4), 25
        )

    def test_func(self):
        self.assertEqual(my_module.func(2, 2), 4)
        self.assertRaises(
            TypeError, my_module.func, "2", 3
        )
        self.assertRaises(
            TypeError, my_module.func, 2, "3"
        )
        self.assertRaises(
            TypeError, my_module.func, "2", "3"
        )

if __name__ == "__main__":
    unittest.main()
```

In order to create our *Test Case*, we must create a subclass of `unittest.TestCase`. Inside the class definition, we create our individual tests, by defining methods with names starting with `test_`. This naming convention is important to inform the test runner about which methods define the actual tests.

On the base of testing are the *assertion* methods. These methods names have `assert` as prefix and fail when an assertion fails. (**Note**: please check the official documentation of `unittest` for a complete list of assertion methods).

When a test fails, an exception will be raised and the test will be identified as a failure. Other exceptions are identified as errors.

So, the **assertEqual** method succeeds if the both arguments evaluate to the same value. On the other hand, **assertRaises** succeeds if calling the callable object (the second argument) with the remaining positional arguments raises an exception of the class specified as the first argument. In other words, as an example, calling **my_module.func** with "2" and 3 should raise a `TypeError` exception.

Let's now run our unit test:

```
→ ~/StartCareerPython python -m unittest —v \
> test_my_module
test_add_numbers (test_my_module.TestMyModule) ... ok
test_func (test_my_module.TestMyModule) ... ok


--------------------------------------------------------
Ran 2 tests in 0.000s

OK
```

The output provides some information, like which tests were run and what was their status. The −v flag is used to add extra verbosity to the output, but it's not mandatory. Let's now change one of the tests and see the different output you get when a test fails.

```
def test_add_numbers(self):
    self.assertEqual(my_module.add_numbers(4, 3), 8)
    self.assertEqual(my_module.add_numbers(3, 4), 24)
```

```
→ ~/StartCareerPython python -m unittest —v \
> test_my_module
test_add_numbers (test_my_module.TestMyModule) ... FAIL
test_func (test_my_module.TestMyModule) ... ok

========================================================
FAIL: test_add_numbers (test_my_module.TestMyModule)
--------------------------------------------------------
Traceback (most recent call last):
 File
"/Users/pmpro/StartCareerPython/test_my_module.py",
line 7, in test_add_numbers
    self.assertEqual(my_module.add_numbers(4, 3), 8)
AssertionError: 7 != 8

--------------------------------------------------------
Ran 2 tests in 0.001s

FAILED (failures=1)
```

At the beginning the amount of information may be a bit overwhelming.

Let's start from the top: two tests were run and **test_add_numbers** was identified with `FAIL`. Below the two tests you have the FAIL reason, with some debugging information. It basically says that the assertion on the line 7 of your file failed because `7 != 8.7` was the result produced by evaluating the expression **my_module.add_numbers(4, 3)**.

In this particular situation, the test failed because the test itself was wrong (on purpose), which means that you need to be a bit careful when writing your own tests, or else you can have a bit of a headache trying to fix your code when in fact your test was broken.

From the command line, you can run tests from modules, classes and individual tests. For example:

```
python -m unittest -v test_my_module
python -m unittest -v test_my_module.TestMyModule
python -m unittest -v
test_my_module.TestMyModule.test_func
```

A way of organizing your test code is through **setUp** and **tearDown** methods. Imagine that there are some operations that you need to do at the beginning of every test. You can put that code in the **setUp** method, which will be called for every single test you have:

```
import unittest

import my_module

class TestMyModule(unittest.TestCase):
    def setUp(self):
        do_something()

    def test_add_numbers(self):
        ...
```

Inside the **setUp** method you can initialize some instance variables like `self.variable = 2` and then use these same variables in your tests.

The counterpart of **setUp** is **tearDown**, which will be run for each test method, whether they have succeeded or not.

```
import unittest

import my_module

class TestMyModule(unittest.TestCase):
    def setUp(self):
        do_something()

    def tearDown(self):
        do_cleanup()

    def test_add_numbers(self):
        ...
```

Even though I just scratched the surface of testing, the truth is that this knowledge is already more than enough to get you started and achieving a good code coverage.

Now the question is: what should I test? Like I said, aim for 100% of coverage, but don't be too fuss about it. Ideally, every critical part of your code should be covered with tests, as well as new functionality that is added.

Don't spend time testing things that were already tested, like external libraries or built-in modules that you may be using.

I've mentioned *coverage* a few times and I haven't explained what it is, even though you may be guessing it correctly. The unit tests you write will invoke a function or method that, most likely, will use other parts of your code. They will *cover* other parts of your code. Of course, two different tests may overlap in the code they cover, which is normal, as long as they don't overlap in 100% of the code, which probably means the tests a redundant.

There is an external library for Python called **nose** that enhances the functionality of `unittest` and provides coverage reports. In section *4.1 pip* I will explain how to install these external libraries.

--- ♦ ---

Summary

And this is the end of Step 2. Hopefully you got your hands dirty as you progressed through the chapter. Actually, the most important thing you can do is try out the examples, experiment, fail, understand why you failed, check the help in the interactive shell and re-read things. Also complement this literature with the official online documentation, if / when needed. Here's a small what you've learned so far:

- Variables are names associated to memory locations where values are stored.
- Python has Numbers data types (such as *int*, *float* and *bool*), Sequences (*str*, *bytes*, *list*, *tuple*, *bytearray*), Sets, Dictionaries, amongst others. Some types are immutable, others are not.
- `if` statements allow you to control of the flow of your program. They can optionally have `elif` and `else` clauses.
- `for` loops allow you to iterate over the elements of an *iterable*. *Iterators* represent streams of data and repeated calls of their **__next__** method successive items in that stream. *Iterables* are objects capable of returning their elements one at a time via an *iterator*.
- A `while` loop executes the statements of its body as long as the expression is evaluated to `True`.
- Functions wrap a block of code and have a name associated, unless they are anonymous (defined with `lambda` expressions).

- File objects expose an API to underlying resources (files), with methods such as read or write. Before performing file operations, you must first open it, and when you're done you close it. You can open files in several different modes.
- Modules are regular files with Python code that contains definitions and statements. Packages are directories that contain a _init_.py file, which can be empty. You can import modules in your code using the `import` statement.
- Exceptions break out the normal flow of your code in order to handle exceptional conditions or errors. You can handle different kinds of exceptions using the `try` statement.
- Object Oriented Programming (OOP) is a programming paradigm based on the interaction between objects. Objects are instances of classes that define state (attributes or properties) and behavior (methods). A class can have subclasses or parent classes.
- Functional Programming is a programming paradigm where computations are treated as evaluation of mathematical functions and avoids side effects and mutable data. Functions are of higher-order and first class citizens. Python provides features and constructs of Functional Programming.

Challenges

Words and weights (part 1)

Given a file with words (a word per line), print a dictionary that maps each word to its *weight*. The *weight* of a word is the sum of each letter's *weight*. The *weight* of a letter is its position in the English alphabet, so a's weight is 1, b is 2 and so on. The weight of a letter is independent of its case, which means that the weight of `a` is the same as the weight of `A`. Assume that each word only contains letters from A to Z (both in lower and uppercase).

Sample input:
```
THISISaveRYLongworD
marKET
anothERLongWORD
```

Sample output:
```
{'THISISaveRYLongworD': 263, 'marKET': 68,
'anothERLongWORD': 189}
```

Hint: `ord("a")`

Words and weights (part 2)

Now, instead of having one word per line, your file has lines with multiple words, separated by commas. You are still supposed to print a dictionary with the words (without any commas, spaces or periods) as keys and their weights as values, but bear in mind that words can be repeated in the file. For words that occur more than once, their value in the dictionary is their weight multiplied by the number of times they occur in the file. Also, for a word to be considered repeated, it doesn't need to match the case. Consider the next line:

```
Lorem,ipsum,dolor,sit,amet,consectetur,adipisc
ing,elit,sed,do,eiusmod,LOREm seD,AMET
```

The words `Lorem`, `sed` and `amet` occur twice. To make things simpler, the words should be stored in the dictionary in lowercase.

Sample input:

```
Lorem,ipsum,dolor,sit,amet,consectetur,adipiscing,e
lit,sed,do,eiusmod,LOREm,seD,AMET
nrwjnen,HELOO,Hello,worl,world,WORLD
dworld,hello,GOOD,mORNIG,MORNING,morning
```

Sample output:
```
{'lorem': 126, 'ipsum': 78, 'sed': 56,
'dolor': 64, 'dworld': 76, 'elit': 46,
'hello': 104, 'world': 144, 'nrwjnen': 98,
'eiusmod': 86, 'do': 19, 'morning': 180,
'consectetur': 143, 'mornig': 76, 'worl':
68, 'sit': 48, 'adipiscing': 91, 'heloo':
55, 'good': 41, 'amet': 78}
```

Stock prices

Someone decided to build a little application that tracks the price of stocks from company XPTO every hour and writes it in a file. The file is made of several lines, each line starting with a date and a colon, followed by at most 8 floating point numbers. Each number represents the price of the stock at the moment it's being written down in the file and each line represents a day. You are now assigned the task of going through the file and printing the following information:

- The difference between the highest and lowest prices ever registered
- For each day, the lowest and highest prices, the difference between the highest and lowest prices, as well as the average price for the day.

The daily information should be organized in a **dictionary**. See the *Sample output* below.

Sample input:
```
1/2/2015: 44.09 43.87 43.90 43.75 43.61 43.55 43.02 42.89
2/2/2015: 42.89 42.97 42.90 42.74 42.70 42.65 42.81 42.83
3/2/2015: 42.83 43.01 43.30 43.24 43.33 43.47 43.50 43.45
4/2/2015: 43.45 43.62 43.68 43.72 43.88 44.02 44.20 44.37
```

Sample output:
```
1.7199999999999989
{'4/2/2015': {'average': 43.8675, 'highest': 44.37,
'difference': 0.9199999999999946, 'lowest': 43.45},
'1/2/2015': {'average': 43.585, 'highest': 44.09,
'difference': 1.2000000000000028, 'lowest': 42.89},
'2/2/2015': {'average': 42.811249999999994,
'highest': 42.97, 'difference': 0.3200000000000003,
'lowest': 42.65}, '3/2/2015': {'average':
43.26624999999999, 'highest': 43.5, 'difference':
0.6700000000000017, 'lowest': 42.83}}
```

The first line is the difference between the highest and lowest prices ever registered.

Hint: if you want to print the dictionary in a nicer way, you can use the function **pprint** from the the built-in module pprint. Import the module in the interactive shell and type **help(pprint.pprint)**.

Step 3 – Using Version Control Systems: Git

Time for a little break! In the previous step, you learned enough to start writing some small apps and were also given enough resources to be a bit more ambitious in your creations. Nonetheless, developing software is not just about writing code.

Note: If you are already an experienced developer or if you have worked with Git or any other Version Control System before, it's safe for you to skip this step. If you have very basic knowledge of Git, stick around as you may learn something new.

Let's say that you start now working on some new project and it's still fairly simple and small and you're happy with it. Suddenly, you think of a potential feature, but you're not sure about it, so you decide to make a copy of your current work and start developing the new feature from there. If you are unhappy with the result or don't feel like continuing because it no longer makes sense, you can just delete the working copy and continue from the previous one. But if you decide to go back to it again, it's lost forever, unless you kept both copies.

As you can imagine, this becomes unmanageable when your application grows in size and complexity. Or imagine that, for instance, you want to have someone helping you develop whatever application you are working on. You'd have to send them the files with your code (and any other assets) either via email or using a USB stick... whatever the solution, it would be far from practical. Especially when you want to merge the changes (which would probably happen on a daily basis).

This is where a special breed of software called *Version Control System* comes in. VCSs make your life, as a developer (and not just as a developer), much easier because of their features and purposes:

- Keep a history of versions of any files it is tracking. Meaning that you can easily retrieve a version from 3 months ago and work on it. And this applies to any file, so if you are a designer and want to keep track of different versions of a logo, for example, you can!

- Facilitate the collaboration between people, by allowing, amongst other things, people to work on the same file without conflicts (well, sort of...but we'll see about this later).

A VCS isn't limited to these two features, but they are amongst the most attractive. Before proceeding, there is an important distinction to make. You have centralized and decentralized VCSs. A centralized VCS keeps everything in one single location (or one single server), whereas with a decentralized VCS every client is a server and contains all the revisions of all the files and everything else.

Note: let me explain what do I mean by *client* and *server*. Again, I don't assume that you know any of these things beforehand. In computing, a *server* refers to a device or a program that provides a service or functionality for other programs or devices to consume it, the *clients*. Take the email example. When you read your emails using Gmail, you are using the web *client* (via web, in your browser) to access the email *server* (or servers) and retrieve your emails. A single computer can be a server for more than one service, as you can imagine. For example, in my computer I am running a database server (MySQL), a web server (NGINX) to serve web pages and many other things.

One of the issues of a centralized VCS is that there is one single point of failure, meaning that if something happens to the server, your files are gone forever. In decentralized VCSs, every client is a server, meaning that any client contains all the revisions of all the files. So if the main server dies, you can still restore it using one of the clients' *repository*.

There are, of course, a few disadvantages when using decentralized VCSs. One of the problems is the large repositories. The problem is actually not having a very large repository on your laptop, per se, but the initial time it takes to *clone* the repository from some other server. Another problem has got to do with administration.

Nonetheless, I cannot even recall how my life was before I started using decentralized VCS, namely *Git*. I believe that I used to perceive the world as a darker place, but not anymore. Without further delay, let's get to the gist!

3.1 Git by example

Git is a free and open source decentralized (and distributed) version control system, that is designed to handle projects with speed and efficiency, no matter their size. There are others, like Mercurial or Bazaar, but in this book I will just cover Git. I won't explain in detail how Git works, but I'll provide enough information for you to understand how to use it.

Before getting started, you should **install**[28] Git. The official documentation is very easy to follow, so you shouldn't have any problem. As soon as you have it installed, head to the command-line (if you weren't there already) and let's get started.

You decided to take your knowledge of Python and programming to another level, so you started a little application that curates the contents of files, for future re-use.

```
→ ~/StartCareerPython mkdir FileCurator
→ ~/StartCareerPython cd FileCurator/
→ ~/StartCareerPython/FileCurator git init
Initialized empty Git repository in
/Users/pmpro/StartCareerPython/FileCurator/.git/
```

The first step is to create a directory and turn it into a Git *repository*. The command `git init` executed inside the newly created **FileCurator** directory does that. The directory right now only has one hidden directory called **.git**, which contains a configuration file and directories that will hold information about the revisions of your files, branches, etc.

Let's create a *main.py* file and see how does this affect our repository:

```
→ ~/StartCareerPython/FileCurator touch main.py

→ ~/StartCareerPython/FileCurator git status
On branch master

Initial commit

Untracked files:
  (use "git add <file>..." to include in what will be
committed)

    main.py

nothing added to commit but untracked files present
(use "git add" to track)
```

Alright, now some background information. In Git (and other VCSs), you work in *branches*. A *branch* is some sort of timeline with the history of changes you've made, in the form of *snapshots*. When you create a Git repository with `git init`, you will be immediately in a branch called `master`. You can have several branches at the same time and switch between them (more on this later).

Now, when you initialized the directory as a repository, it was empty (except for the hidden **.git** directory, created by the command itself). Afterwards, a new file was created. Every file in your working directory is either *tracked* or *untracked*. A file is tracked when it makes part of the last snapshot. Tracked files are also *unmodified*, *modified* or *staged*.

Let's go back one step to the *tracked* vs *untracked* state. The command `git status` shows which file is on which state in the current branch. The current branch is *master* and we have one untracked file: *main.py*. It also says that if we want the file to be tracked, we must run the command `git add main.py`. So let's do it!

```
➜  ~/StartCareerPython/FileCurator git add main.py
➜  ~/StartCareerPython/FileCurator git status
On branch master

Initial commit

Changes to be committed:
  (use "git rm --cached <file>..." to unstage)

    new file:   main.py
```

The file *main.py* is now *tracked* **and** *staged*, meaning that it's ready to be added to the next *commit*. In Git terminology, *committing* means to record your changes to the branch. It's like taking a snapshot of the current state of the branch and saving it. You do so with the command `git commit`. The flag `-m` allows you to add a commit message, ideally something relevant so that it provides good information when someone is browsing the commit history.

```
➜  ~/StartCareerPython/FileCurator git commit -m
↵ "My first commit"
[master (root-commit) a70e5bd] My first commit
1 file changed, 0 insertions(+), 0 deletions(-)
create mode 100644 main.py
```

```
→ ~/StartCareerPython/FileCurator  git status
On branch master
nothing to commit, working directory clean
```

There, everything is committed! Another important concept in Git is the *pointer*. Every time you commit changes, Git creates a commit object that contains a *pointer* to the snapshot of the content, your name, email, the commit message and a pointer (or pointers) to the commit or commits that came immediately before.

A commit is identified by a *checksum*, which is a hexadecimal number that results from applying the hash function *SHA-1* to the files and subdirectories of your project. Don't worry much about it, just keep in mind that each commit is uniquely identified by a hexadecimal number. Let's run the command `git log`, to see the history of the commits:

```
→ ~/StartCareerPython/FileCurator git log
commit a70e5bd88e4271a340130cb33b96ef3b023c5af5
Author: Pedro Rodrigues <-----@-----.com>
Date:   Thu Jul 28 16:54:43 2016 +0200

    My first commit
```

There is only one commit, made by me at a certain date, with a certain message and identified by a certain checksum. Let's modify the file *main.py* and add some code:

```
# -*- coding: utf-8 -*-

SOURCE_FILE = "file_to_curate.txt"
# Curated file name will be file_to_curate.cur
CURATED_FILE = SOURCE_FILE.split(".")[0] + ".cur"

def curate_string(string):
    """
    Receives a string and curates it in a certain way.
    :param string: The string to be curated
    :return: The curated string
```

```
    :rtype : str
    """

    return string  # to do

with open(SOURCE_FILE) as source,
    open(CURATED_FILE, "w") as curated:
    for line in source:
        curated.write(curate_string(line))
```

Here's what `git status` tells us this time:

```
→ ~/StartCareerPython/FileCurator  git status
On branch master
Changes not staged for commit:
  (use "git add <file>..." to update what will be
committed)
  (use "git checkout -- <file>..." to discard changes in
working directory)

    modified:   main.py

no changes added to commit (use "git add" and/or "git
commit -a")
```

The file is *tracked,* but *modified* and still not *staged*. Which means that if you tried to commit right now, the changes wouldn't be recorded:

```
→ ~/StartCareerPython/FileCurator  git commit —m
↵ "Trying to commit with modified files"
On branch master
Changes not staged for commit:
    modified:   main.py

no changes added to commit
```

Let's stage the file, commit and check the history:

```
→ ~/StartCareerPython/FileCurator  git add main.py

→ ~/StartCareerPython/FileCurator  git commit —m
```

```
⏎ "Initial code that reads from the source file and
creates a new curated file"
[master 219b273] Initial code that reads from the
source file and creates a new curated file
1 file changed, 19 insertions(+)


→ ~/StartCareerPython/FileCurator  git log
commit 219b27340db1f9d22469bfe4c0845a012eaefcba
Author: Pedro Rodrigues <----@----.com>
Date:   Fri Jul 28 19:25:56 2016 +0200

    Initial code that reads from the source file and
creates a new curated file

commit a70e5bd88e4271a340130cb33b96ef3b023c5af5
Author: Pedro Rodrigues <----@----.com>
Date:   Thu Jul 28 16:54:43 2016 +0200

    My first commit
```

The branch `master` has two commit objects, each with a
pointer to the respective snapshot.

Now that you have enough background information, I can
give you a definition of branch that is closer to reality: a branch
is a moving pointer in a timeline of commit objects. Every time
you commit, the pointer moves to the last commit. There is
also another special pointer called `HEAD`, that points to the
current working branch. This is how Git knows which branch
we're currently working on.

Let's say that we are happy with the current code we have,
but there is a new feature we want to add and test it
separately. We can create a new branch from `master` and
work there. Let's call this branch `new-feature`:

```
→ ~/StartCareerPython/FileCurator  git branch
⏎ new-feature
```

The `git branch` command only created the new branch,
but it didn't switch to it. You can confirm that you're still in the

`master` branch with `git status`. To switch to the new branch, we use `git checkout`:

```
→ ~/StartCareerPython/FileCurator git checkout
↵ new-feature
Switched to branch 'new-feature'
```

So, when you created the new branch, you actually created a new moving pointer called `new-feature` that is pointing to the same commit object as `master`. When you switch to the new branch, the pointer `HEAD` points to it. Note that right now the two branches share the same commit history:

```
→ ~/StartCareerPython/FileCurator  git log
commit 219b27340db1f9d22469bfe4c0845a012eaefcba
Author: Pedro Rodrigues <----@----.com>
Date:   Fri Jul 29 19:25:56 2016 +0200

    Initial code that reads from the source file and
creates a new curated file

commit a70e5bd88e4271a340130cb33b96ef3b023c5af5
Author: Pedro Rodrigues <----@----.com>
Date:   Thu Jul 28 16:54:43 2016 +0200

    My first commit
```

The two timelines overlap until you start making changes in the new branch. From that point onwards, the commits will diverge. Also, when you switch branches, you are also changing the contents of your working directory. Let's see that by creating a new file, staging, committing and then switching back to master:

```
→ ~/StartCareerPython/FileCurator  touch curators.py

→ ~/StartCareerPython/FileCurator  git add curators.py

→ ~/StartCareerPython/FileCurator  git commit -m
```

```
⏎ "Added a module for curators"
[new-feature ede0b3f] Added a module for curators
1 file changed, 0 insertions(+), 0 deletions(-)
create mode 100644 curators.py

→ ~/StartCareerPython/FileCurator   ls
curators.py  main.py
```

There are two files in the current directory and the commit history contains 3 commit objects. Run the command `git log` to confirm it. Let's now switch back to `master` and check the contents of the directory and the commit log:

```
→ ~/StartCareerPython/FileCurator   git checkout master
Switched to branch 'master'

→ ~/StartCareerPython/FileCurator   ls
main.py

→ ~/StartCareerPython/FileCurator   git log
commit 219b27340db1f9d22469bfe4c0845a012eaefcba
Author: Pedro Rodrigues <----@----.com>
Date:   Fri Jul 29 19:25:56 2016 +0200

    Initial code that reads from the source file and
creates a new curated file

commit a70e5bd88e4271a340130cb33b96ef3b023c5af5
Author: Pedro Rodrigues <----@----.com>
Date:   Thu Jul 28 16:54:43 2016 +0200

    My first commit
```

What if you are happy with your new feature and want to merge the changes into `master`? Well, that's where `git merge` comes in:

```
→ ~/StartCareerPython/FileCurator git merge --no-ff
⏎ new-feature -m "Merged the curators module into
master"
Merge made by the 'recursive' strategy.
curators.py | 1 +
1 file changed, 1 insertion(+)
```

The flag `--no-ff` is a short for *no fast forward*. When passing this flag, a merge commit is created, instead of just updating pointer. Even though this flag is not mandatory, it's quite useful when you want to have a model based on feature branches (which was the case). Using `--no-ff` will treat the feature branch and its commits as one single unit.

When you want to merge a branch A into a branch B, you must first switch to branch B and then invoke `git merge -m <message>` A. Run `git log` and inspect the output.

Even though it's outside the scope of this book to go into detailed explanations about Git, there are still three commands worth explaining. For the rest, you should check the *Pro Git*[29] book, which is freely available online.

git clone

The above scenario involved you creating your own repository and working on it. What if you wanted to work on someone else's project? Remember that with Git every *client* involved has a full copy of the repository (hence the decentralization), which means that first you would have to *clone* the repository into your laptop before starting to work. You do this with `git clone`. For example, let's suppose that you want to help your friend Laura work on her project, which is hosted in her server at http://lauraserver.com/project. In order to clone the repository to your machine, you would just do `git clone http://lauraserver.com/project`. After that, you would use the commands explained above.

Nonetheless, the changes you'd made would only be available in your local copy of the repository. So how can you make those changes available for everyone?

git push is the answer to the previous question. After a commit (which records the changes in your local branch), you need to push the changes to the *origin*. *Origin* is the default name that Git gives to the server you cloned from, in this case Laura's server. So, if you want to push the changes made in your local master branch, you do git push origin master.

Now anyone who joins the project and clones the repository will have your latest changes. But what about people who are already working on it? Do they have to clone the repository again? Of course not! The answer comes right away.

They pull the changes from the *origin*! So, if Laura wants to merge the changes you've pushed into master, she would just need to switch to her local master branch and run git pull.

3.2 Hosted Git repositories: GitHub

There are several places where you can host your own Git repositories, but **GitHub**[30] is the largest one. You can create a free account and innumerous repositories, facilitating collaboration between developers. It's also an amazing way of showing off your portfolio. Companies and individuals use GitHub not just for hosting their projects, but also for code review, issue tracking, etc. Again, I urge you to explore the online version of the book *Pro Git*[29], which also has an entire chapter dedicated to properly use GitHub.

Step 4 – Getting practical with Python

What you've learned in Step 2 is enough to get you started and gives you the necessary foundations to go far, but in order to go far you need to walk the walk. In this Step, I will show you a few directions you can take, some things that are worth taking a look at and hopefully spark a bit more curiosity in you.

4.1 pip

Developing software is about using existing building blocks to create something new, sometimes new building blocks to be used by someone else. The last thing you want is to constantly reinvent the wheel, unless you have a really good reason for it (which you probably won't have at the beginning).

Reusing existing libraries or frameworks has lots of advantages, mainly because they have already been tested (hopefully) and used by more people. Python has something called *pip* (a recursive acronym that stands for "*Pip Installs Packages*"), which is a package management system that you can use to install and manage... packages. If you installed Python following the installation instructions in python.org then you already have *pip*. Sometimes, the *pip* for Python 3 is called *pip3* instead. In your terminal enter `pip --version` and hopefully it will show something similar to this:

```
→ ~ pip --version
pip 8.1.2 from
/opt/local/Library/Frameworks/Python.framework/Versions
/3.5/lib/python3.5/site-packages (python 3.5)

→ ~
```

If the version isn't associated to your Python 3.5.*, then try with pip3 instead. Like I've mentioned in the note at the beginning of *Step 2*, the Python version matters because you may be trying to search or install a package that is not available for your version of Python.

In order to see what available commands *pip* has, just type `pip` in the command line and press Enter. The commands I use the most are `install`, `uninstall` and `search`. Let's see a practical example. In section *2.10 Testing your code* I briefly mentioned **nose**, a library that enhances the functionalities of `unittest`. Well, let's install it! First, enter the command `pip search nose`:

```
→ ~ pip search nose
...
...
nose (1.3.7)                    - nose extends unittest to
                                  make testing easier
...
...
```

The 3 dots there are just to indicate that there are more search results, but the one we are interested in is `nose (1.3.7)`. In the search result, you will see the name of the package on the left and the latest version between parentheses. On the right hand side there is a brief description of the functionalities that the package provides. And now we install it:

```
→ ~ sudo pip install nose
Password:
Collecting nose
 Cache entry deserialization failed, entry ignored
 Downloading nose-1.3.7-py3-none-any.whl (154kB)
   100% |████████████████████████████████| 163kB 1.9MB/s
Installing collected packages: nose
Successfully installed nose-1.3.7

→ ~
```

You will probably have to precede the command with `sudo`, in order to run it with *superuser* privileges, or else you won't be able to install the package in the default location. And that's it, the package was installed. Let's confirm, by importing it in the interactive shell:

```
>>> import nose
>>> dir(nose)
['DeprecatedTest', 'SkipTest', '__all__', '__author__',
'__builtins__', '__cached__', '__doc__', '__file__',
'__loader__', '__name__', '__package__', '__path__',
'__spec__', '__version__', '__versioninfo__', 'case',
'collector', 'config', 'core', 'exc', 'failure',
'importer', 'loader', 'main', 'plugins', 'proxy',
'pyversion', 'result', 'run', 'run_exit', 'runmodule',
'sector', 'suite', 'tools', 'util', 'with_setup']
```

That's it, you're ready to rock! If you want to uninstall nose, you simply enter the command `pip uninstall nose` in the command line. Because these packages are usually under constant development, you may want to upgrade them to the latest version. You do it by running the command `pip install --upgrade <package_name>` (you would replace <package_name> with nose, in this case).

4.2 REST and RESTful APIs

Web services are a good way to retrieve data that you can later manipulate because the data is usually relevant for what you want to do and properly formatted.

A Web Service is a service that is provided by an electronic device to another device, via Web. If you recall the City Hall example in section *1.6.1 IP Address, localhost and port*, the Taxes service can be seen as a Web service and you as its consumer. Web Services vary in the way they provide the services, or in the way they "speak" with the clients that consume them. There are standards that specify these protocols and detail how can the Web Services be found, what should be the format of a request and of a response, etc.

A Web Service that uses **REST** architecture is often called a **RESTful** (or **REST**) **API**. REST stands for **RE**presentational **S**tate **T**ransfer, which is an architectural style for designing and developing networked applications. This architectural style relies on a *stateless* and *cacheable* communications protocol between a client and a server. *Stateless* means that no client context is stored on the server between requests, which means that every request that the client performs on the server must contain all the necessary information for the request to be fulfilled by the server. As for cacheable...

Well, let's go back to the Taxes service once again. The City Hall has a RESTful API for the Taxes service, that allows you to perform certain requests to it, for example ask whether your taxes situation is up to date. So, once again, you arrive at the door of the City Hall with your request (written in a piece of paper) and deliver it to Mr. Kernel, who in turn delivers to the Taxes department. The employee in the Taxes department takes the request and understands that you want to check your current situation. She doesn't know it by heart, so she goes to the computer to check it, taking a couple of seconds and then gives a response with the information you need to Mr. Kernel, who in turn forwards it to you. A few seconds later, you return to the City Hall and make the exact same request, but this time the response comes much faster, because the employee in the Taxes department still remembered the response she had sent you. She didn't have to go to the computer and check it, she just responded right away. The response was *cached*.

Often, but not always, the HTTP protocol is used for RESTful APIs.

So for this particular example, you could have performed an HTTP request to an *endpoint* like:

http://cityhall.com/taxes?action=query&citizen=12345&format=json

I just made it up. What you see in this URI (*Uniform Resource Identifier*) after the question mark is what is called *query parameters*. There are three parameters, in this case: `action` (with value `query`), `citizen` (with value `12345`) and `format` (with value `json`). `taxes` identifies the resource in the City Hall. `format=json` indicates that you want the response to be sent in **JSON** (JavaScript Object Notation) format. The **JSON**[31] format actually resembles Python dictionaries a lot. Let's see a practical example of a client consuming a RESTful API. For that, I will be using a publicly available API from Wikipedia and the built-in module `urllib` to consume it. You can find more information about Wikipedia's public API **here**[32], but it basically provides a convenient access to features, data and metadata of Wikipedia pages.

```python
import urllib.parse
import urllib.request

url = "https://en.wikipedia.org/w/api.php"

# key/value pairs to be used as query parameters
values = {
    "action": "query",
    "titles": "CPython",
    "prop": "revisions",
    "format": "json"
}

# ?action=query&titles=CPython&prop=revisions&format=json
data = urllib.parse.urlencode(values)
# query params may only contain ASCII
data = data.encode("ascii")
request = urllib.request.Request(url, data)
with urllib.request.urlopen(request) as response:
    the_page = response.read()

print(the_page)
```

(file rest_api1.py)

```
➜ ~/StartCareerPython python rest_api1.py
b'{"batchcomplete":"","query":{"pages":{"1984246":{"pag
eid":1984246,"ns":0,"title":"CPython","revisions":[{"re
vid":729615721,"parentid":729557045,"user":"Codename
Lisa","timestamp":"2016-07-
13T12:25:44Z","comment":"Reverted [[WP:AGF|good faith]]
edits by
[[Special:Contributions/Jasonanaggie|Jasonanaggie]]
([[User talk:Jasonanaggie|talk]])."}]}}}}'
```

Before I explain, can you make sense out of the code? Well, I didn't guess what query parameters are accepted by Wikipedia's API, I had to read the documentation. They have an explanation with the purpose of each parameter. The `urllib` module provides lots of functionality for performing HTTP requests and parsing the responses in an easy fashion. So my aim is to perform an HTTP request with a GET method to the URL:

https://en.wikipedia.org/w/api.php?action=query&titles=CPython&prop=revisions&format=json

The **urlencode** method takes care of returning a string with the query parameters properly formatted. Afterwards, I am encoding the string to ASCII because URLs cannot contain non-ASCII characters. Finally, I am building a request object based on the base URL and the query parameters string. Note that I am able to use the object returned by **urlopen** in the with statement because it provides a *context manager*. The rest is quite straightforward. Make sure you read the *HOWTO Fetch Internet Resources Using the urllib Package*[33], from the official documentation.

What if you want to write your own RESTful API, how would you do it? Well, there are several open source projects out there that provide lots of abstractions and make your life easy, so building a RESTful API is a piece of cake. Some of them are quite slim and compact, others involve a bigger learning curve, but it all depends on how complex you want your application to be. There is **Django**[34], **Flask**[35], **Werkzeug**[36], **Tornado**[37], you name it!

I will be using Flask for this example, because it's extremely compact and I don't have to setup anything. Let's start by getting it from *pip*, using `sudo pip install flask` (it will automatically install a few dependencies before). And now let's write some code! Let's create an *endpoint* for the Taxes service in a file called *taxes.py*. This endpoint will only accept the HTTP method GET:

```python
from flask import Flask, request, jsonify
app = Flask(__name__)


@app.route('/taxes')
def taxes():
    """
    This is our handler for
    http://whatever:5000/taxes?...

    It accepts the following query parameters:
    action, citizen and (response) format.
    By default, action is query and format is json.
    """
    action = request.args.get("action", "query")
    citizen = request.args.get("citizen", "")
    _format = request.args.get("format", "json")

    response = {
        "action": action,
        "citizen": citizen,
        "situation": "On time",
    }

    if _format == "json":
        return jsonify(**response)
    else:
        return "I don't know that format!!!"
```

(file taxes.py)

Can you understand the code? It's not that hard, right? In the second line we are creating an instance of Flask class, which will be our **WSGI** application. I didn't guess it, I just read in the documentation how to do it.

Note: **WSGI** (*Web Server Gateway Interface*) is a specification for interface between web servers and web applications for Python. There are two sides involved in this specification: the server (which is a web server like Apache or Nginx) and the web application or framework itself (which is the Python code). You can read more about it in the Wikipedia **entry**[38].

`request` is a global object that represents an HTTP request received by our Flask application. It contains an `args` property, which is a dictionary with the query parameters. The method **get** is being used with two parameters to avoid `KeyError` exception (raised when you try to retrieve a nonexistent key from a dictionary): the second parameter is a default value in case the key doesn't exist. The function **jsonify** is used to send a JSON response.

Now let's run this little app in the command line. If you check Flask's *documentation*[39], you'll see that you can run your application in several ways. Let's now go to the command-line:

```
→ ~/StartCareerPython export FLASK_APP=taxes.py

→ ~/StartCareerPython python -m flask run
* Serving Flask app "taxes"
* Running on http://127.0.0.1:5000/ (Press CTRL+C to quit)
```

We just created an environment variable `FLASK_APP` with a value that is the name of our Python script. Note that our application will be listening by default on port 5000. Time to go to the browser!

Let's start by entering **http://127.0.0.1:5000/taxes** in the search bar. You will get a response with the default values:

Try to add now a value for the citizen query parameter: **http://127.0.0.1:5000/taxes?citizen=john**.

{
    "action": "query",
    "citizen": "john",
    "situation": "On time"
}

Awesome! It's now your turn to make experiments. Also change the code, add more handlers for different endpoints, etc!

4.3 Python and Storage

Even though you've learned how to manipulate files, you shouldn't be using them to store complex data. Better yet, you shouldn't invent ways of manipulating complex data stored in a file. The reason why I rephrased is because databases store data in files, but they provide ways and abstractions for you to manipulate the data in a secure and efficient fashion.

> **Note**: it's not always true that databases store data in files. Sometimes the data may just stay in main memory, for faster access, and won't be stored in files. This is often the case when you use a database like Redis as cache, even though you are given the option to store the data. It also means that when you shut down the database server (or if it dies for some reason) the data is lost.

There are several databases available which you can download and play with, but it will involve a bit of learning upfront.

Databases like MySQL or PostgreSQL are said to be relational databases, because they allow you to store and organize data in a way that it expresses the existing relationships. The SQL (*Structured Query Language*) standard is a specification for a query language that allows you to manipulate data stored in such databases. Different databases implement their own version of the SQL standard, which are mostly compatible amongst themselves.

Then you have another breed of databases, called NoSQL, which are mostly known for being fast and flexible (they don't require fixed table schemas), as well as designed to *scale horizontally*.

> **Note**: to scale horizontally means to add more nodes or servers (or removing) to a distributed application or system. For example, if you have a single database server in a node (a node refers to a computer) and you add another node with that same database server (which won't store the same data as the first one, most likely) you are scaling out horizontally. This is a common scenario when the data you are storing grows above a certain size or when you want to distribute the load between more servers. This also means that the management and configuration complexity of the nodes grows as well, alongside with the complexity of the programming model of your application.

Examples of such databases are MongoDB, CouchDB, Redis or Cassandra. When you are working in a certain application that involves data storage, chances are that there is already at least one database server configured and up and running (this was already taken care by a *DevOps* or *Systems Administrator*... or you).

Nonetheless, it's often useful for you to have a database server running in your own laptop for testing purposes (if you are offline for some reason, you won't be able to connect to a remote database server, right?). (**Note**: It's outside the scope of this book to teach you how to install and configure databases, or to cover the topic. But there is plenty of information, articles and good documentation online that will guide you through the process).

With or without the database server running in your local machine, you will need to have a Python *client* for the specific database you want to connect. These clients are nothing but libraries that provide abstractions, classes, functions and methods to interact with the database and you can import them as modules in your code. Let me show you a little example using Redis client for Python. Note that I already have Redis server running in my local machine:

```
>>> import redis
>>> connection = redis.StrictRedis(host="127.0.0.1",
port=6379)
>>> connection.set("key1", "Value1")
True
>>> connection.get("key1")
b'Value1'
```

The second line is where I connect to my local Redis server. Then I create a new entry, identified by the string `key1` and with a value associated, also a string: `Value1`. The method **connection.set** returns `True` when it succeeds on storing a value. After that, I retrieve the value previously stored, just by referring to its key.

Of course that you could do this with a dictionary, but if you want to share information between services, especially if they are running in different computers, then this is the way to go (or one of the best ways). Redis provides much more functionality than this, of course. Start exploring different databases, install them on your local machine, find the respective Python clients using *pip* (or Google), read the documentation of both the clients and the databases and then start to play around with it.

4.4 Developing for Raspberry Pi

Chances are that you've heard about Raspberry Pi. If you haven't, Raspberry Pi is a credit card-sized computer that was created in the United Kingdom to promote and facilitate the teaching of Computer Science in schools. It used to run just Linux as its Operating System, but at the time of this writing even Windows 10 is available.

Python is promoted as its official development language, but others are supported as well (like C, C++, Java or PHP). You can very easily connect electronic sensors (like temperature or light) or some other devices to your Raspberry Pi and make cool stuff with it.

There are several Python libraries available that let you manipulate whatever you connect there, and you can also write your own. It's completely out of the scope of this book to go further, but there are several resources and books available that will get you started in no time, specially because now you are already acquainted with Python! The best way to start is in the official website of **Raspberry Pi**[40].

4.5 Python for Data Science and Finance

What else can you do with Python? Lots of things! Python's application in real-world is not limited to the topics exposed in this book, but I'm here just to whet your appetite and curiosity. I'm showing you some of the paths available, it's up to you to find the rest.

Python is widely (but not exclusively) used in Finance, mostly by investment banks. Due to its ease of programming, you can very easily write your models and verify their correctness, perform data analysis, etc. Nonetheless, C++ and Java are still the language of choice when speed and performance are mandatory. There are several Python libraries for Finance such as **NumPy**[41], **SciPy**[42] and **Pandas**[43], that allow Quantitative Analysts to perform all sorts of data analysis.

Step 5 – Becoming a better software developer or "where to go from here?"

That's it, you've finished the 4 main steps of the book. You were exposed to the most important concepts of Computer Science to get you started (numeral systems, CPU and Memory, Data Structures and Computer Networking), even though not in depth. After that you became familiar with Python and, if you practiced as you read, hopefully you are now comfortable reading other people's code and writing some useful applications with a certain degree of complexity (I'm not expecting you to finish the book and start writing the next WhatsApp or Facebook...but who knows). You also learned how to use Version Control Systems when developing software and now you are aware of some real life applications of Python. So, what now?

5.1 Start your own project

One of the best ways for you to become a better developer is to... write code! Maybe you already have some idea in mind of an application, so why not start it right now? This will force you to think, make mistakes and learn from them. You will be facing problems and challenges that will force you to research for good solutions and practices. **StackOverflow**[44] is a great community for you to ask for help (and eventually help others).

The more you practice, the more proficient you will become at foreseeing certain scenarios that would otherwise result into future headaches. And during the process, take the chance to read code from other people. In **GitHub**[30] you can find lots of source code from individuals or companies, some with mediocre quality but others are authentic masterpieces of software. It's worth reading and learn how to properly test, document and structure your code.

5.2 Master your toolset

Maybe Python is your first language, but you shouldn't stop here. As you progress, you will hear about lots of different languages, databases, frameworks, libraries, etc. Whatever becomes part of your daily toolset (either by necessity or by choice), make sure to master it. Read all the documentation. Go crazy and even read some of the source code (or all of it, if you have the time).

I remember that back when I started using Linux more than 16 years ago, the documentation online was not abundant as it is right now. When the *man pages*, IRC channels or newsgroups were not enough, we'd have to dive head first into the code. Understand how it works behind the scenes and you will become a ninja! *"Use the Force, read the source!"*

5.3 Keep yourself up-to-date

Even if you don't adopt or use every single new framework and library that comes out, it's always good to be up-to-date. See what other people are using and also see how other people are doing things. There are plenty of blogs or Twitter accounts that are worth following and checking regularly. **Python Weekly**[45] is a good starting point, where you can receive regular emails with the latest curated articles, books, job offers, etc.

Another good way for you to keep yourself up-to-date and expand your knowledge is by taking online courses. **Coursera**[46] is filled with plenty of good (and free) online courses.

5.4 Programming Challenges and Competitions

Online programming challenges and competitions will help you exercise your mental elasticity. You'll be solving most of the times problems from different fields of Computer Science or Math. Not only will this expose you to new concepts but it will also force you to do research during your journey, thus expanding your knowledge.

My favorite sources for online challenges and competitions are **Project Euler**[47] (mostly focused on Math), **CodeEval**[48] (lots of problems in three categories - easy, medium and hard), **HackerRank**[49] (problems vary not only in difficulty but also in field of Computer Science), **CheckIO**[50] (a game that helps you improve your coding skills) and **CodeChef**[51] (with lots of programming challenges and competitions).

5.5 Contributing to Open Source Projects

Another good way for you to become a better developer is to contribute to open source projects. Many people and companies put their projects on the wild, completely available for other people to download and use for free (perhaps with some restrictions, depending on the license), and eventually help. The help can come in the form of bug fixes, writing or translating documentation, development of new features, donations, you name it. The first three ways of contributing we'll help you improve your programming skills. You can even contribute to the Python community and to CPython interpreter itself.

Appendix A. ASCII Characters

Char	Dec	Oct	Hex	Char	Dec	Oct	Hex	Char	Dec	Oct	Hex	Char	Dec	Oct	Hex
(nul)	0	0000	0x00	(sp)	32	0040	0x20	@	64	0100	0x40	`	96	0140	0x60
(soh)	1	0001	0x01	!	33	0041	0x21	A	65	0101	0x41	a	97	0141	0x61
(stx)	2	0002	0x02	"	34	0042	0x22	B	66	0102	0x42	b	98	0142	0x62
(etx)	3	0003	0x03	#	35	0043	0x23	C	67	0103	0x43	c	99	0143	0x63
(eot)	4	0004	0x04	$	36	0044	0x24	D	68	0104	0x44	d	100	0144	0x64
(enq)	5	0005	0x05	%	37	0045	0x25	E	69	0105	0x45	e	101	0145	0x65
(ack)	6	0006	0x06	&	38	0046	0x26	F	70	0106	0x46	f	102	0146	0x66
(bel)	7	0007	0x07	'	39	0047	0x27	G	71	0107	0x47	g	103	0147	0x67
(bs)	8	0010	0x08	(	40	0050	0x28	H	72	0110	0x48	h	104	0150	0x68
(ht)	9	0011	0x09	)	41	0051	0x29	I	73	0111	0x49	i	105	0151	0x69
(nl)	10	0012	0x0a	*	42	0052	0x2a	J	74	0112	0x4a	j	106	0152	0x6a
(vt)	11	0013	0x0b	+	43	0053	0x2b	K	75	0113	0x4b	k	107	0153	0x6b
(np)	12	0014	0x0c	,	44	0054	0x2c	L	76	0114	0x4c	l	108	0154	0x6c
(cr)	13	0015	0x0d	-	45	0055	0x2d	M	77	0115	0x4d	m	109	0155	0x6d
(so)	14	0016	0x0e	.	46	0056	0x2e	N	78	0116	0x4e	n	110	0156	0x6e
(si)	15	0017	0x0f	/	47	0057	0x2f	O	79	0117	0x4f	o	111	0157	0x6f
(dle)	16	0020	0x10	0	48	0060	0x30	P	80	0120	0x50	p	112	0160	0x70
(dc1)	17	0021	0x11	1	49	0061	0x31	Q	81	0121	0x51	q	113	0161	0x71
(dc2)	18	0022	0x12	2	50	0062	0x32	R	82	0122	0x52	r	114	0162	0x72
(dc3)	19	0023	0x13	3	51	0063	0x33	S	83	0123	0x53	s	115	0163	0x73
(dc4)	20	0024	0x14	4	52	0064	0x34	T	84	0124	0x54	t	116	0164	0x74
(nak)	21	0025	0x15	5	53	0065	0x35	U	85	0125	0x55	u	117	0165	0x75
(syn)	22	0026	0x16	6	54	0066	0x36	V	86	0126	0x56	v	118	0166	0x76
(etb)	23	0027	0x17	7	55	0067	0x37	W	87	0127	0x57	w	119	0167	0x77
(can)	24	0030	0x18	8	56	0070	0x38	X	88	0130	0x58	x	120	0170	0x78
(em)	25	0031	0x19	9	57	0071	0x39	Y	89	0131	0x59	y	121	0171	0x79
(sub)	26	0032	0x1a	:	58	0072	0x3a	Z	90	0132	0x5a	z	122	0172	0x7a
(esc)	27	0033	0x1b	;	59	0073	0x3b	[	91	0133	0x5b	{	123	0173	0x7b
(fs)	28	0034	0x1c	<	60	0074	0x3c	\	92	0134	0x5c	|	124	0174	0x7c
(gs)	29	0035	0x1d	=	61	0075	0x3d	]	93	0135	0x5d	}	125	0175	0x7d
(rs)	30	0036	0x1e	>	62	0076	0x3e	^	94	0136	0x5e	~	126	0176	0x7e
(us)	31	0037	0x1f	?	63	0077	0x3f	_	95	0137	0x5f	(del)	127	0177	0x7f

References

1. *How to Become a Hacker*
http://www.catb.org/esr/faqs/hacker-howto.html

2. *Tree data structures*
https://en.wikipedia.org/wiki/Tree_(data_structure)

3. *Application Layer Protocols*
https://en.wikipedia.org/wiki/Application_layer

4. Python download
https://www.python.org/downloads/

5. *Floating Point Arithmetics: Issues and Limitations*
https://docs.python.org/3.5/tutorial/floatingpoint.html

6. *Built-in Types*
https://docs.python.org/3.5/library/stdtypes.html

7. *PEP8*
https://www.python.org/dev/peps/pep-0008/

8. *Text Sequence Types - str*
https://docs.python.org/3.5/library/stdtypes.html#textseq

9. *Objects Values and Types*
https://docs.python.org/3/reference/datamodel.html#objects-values-and-types

10. *Operator Precedence*
https://docs.python.org/3/reference/expressions.html#operator-precedence

11. Vim Adventures
http://vim-adventures.com/

12. *Truth Value Testing*
https://docs.python.org/3.5/library/stdtypes.html#truth-value-testing

13. *Iterator Types*
https://docs.python.org/3.5/library/stdtypes.html#iterator-types

14. open official documentation
https://docs.python.org/3.5/library/functions.html#open

15. The try statement
https://docs.python.org/3/reference/compound_stmts.html#the-try-statement

16. The raise statement
https://docs.python.org/3/reference/simple_stmts.html#the-raise-statement

17. *Built-in Exceptions*
https://docs.python.org/3.5/library/exceptions.html

18. *Errors and Exceptions*
https://docs.python.org/3.5/tutorial/errors.html

19. PYTHONPATH (Environment Variables)
https://docs.python.org/3.5/using/cmdline.html#envvar-PYTHONPATH

20. *Modules*
https://docs.python.org/3.5/tutorial/modules.html

21. The import statement
https://docs.python.org/3/reference/simple_stmts.html#the-import-statement

22. Property class
https://docs.python.org/3/library/functions.html#property

23. The **super** function
https://docs.python.org/3/library/functions.html#super

24. *Design Patterns: Elements of Reusable Object Oriented Software*
https://www.amazon.com/Design-Patterns-Elements-Reusable-Object-Oriented-ebook/dp/B000SEIBB8

25. *Special Method Names*
https://docs.python.org/3/reference/datamodel.html#specialnames

26. *Python Frequently Asked Questions*
https://docs.python.org/3/faq/programming.html#why-do-lambdas-defined-in-a-loop-with-different-values-all-return-the-same-result

27. *Python Functional Programming HOW-TO*
https://docs.python.org/3/howto/functional.html

28. *Installing Git (Pro Git online book)*
https://git-scm.com/book/en/v2/Getting-Started-Installing-Git

29. *Pro Git* online book
https://git-scm.com/book/en/v2

30. **GitHub**
https://github.com/

31. **JSON** *format*
https://en.wikipedia.org/wiki/JSON

32. *Wikipedia'sAPI reference*
https://www.mediawiki.org/wiki/API:Main_page

33. *HOW TO Fetch Internet Resources using the urllib Package*
https://docs.python.org/3/howto/urllib2.html

34. **Django**
https://www.djangoproject.com/

35. **Flask**
http://flask.pocoo.org/

36. **Werkzeug**
http://werkzeug.pocoo.org/

37. **Tornado**
http://www.tornadoweb.org/en/stable/

38. *WSGI (Web Server Gateway Interface) Wikipedia Entry*
https://en.wikipedia.org/wiki/Web_Server_Gateway_Interface

39. *Flask Quickstart guide*
http://flask.pocoo.org/docs/0.11/quickstart/#a-minimal-application

40. Raspberry Pi
https://www.raspberrypi.org/

41. NumPy
http://www.numpy.org/

42. SciPy
https://www.scipy.org/

43. Pandas
http://pandas.pydata.org/

44. StackOverflow
http://stackoverflow.com/

45. Python Weekly
http://www.pythonweekly.com/

46. Coursera
https://www.coursera.org/

47. Project Euler
https://projecteuler.net/archives

48. CodeEval
https://www.codeeval.com/

49. HackerRank
https://www.hackerrank.com/

50. CheckIO
https://checkio.org/

51. CodeChef

https://www.codechef.com/

About the Author

My interest in computers started by the age of 7, when my father bought our very first computer, a Schneider EuroPC. It came with a monochrome monitor and a keyboard with a floppy disk drive embedded in it. I became interested in computer programming thanks to an old Football Manager game written in BASIC, at the beginning of the 90s. My idea was to make changes to the game so that my team would always win. Of course, the game eventually became less interesting.

My passion for programming grew bigger and I eventually started writing some small applications just for the fun, mostly to automate boring tasks. In the late 90s I started playing around with Linux and many times was forced to read source code, since documentation in general at the time was not as abundant as it is today. I eventually enrolled in a Computer Science and Engineering course from which I graduated a few years later, but most of my knowledge about computers and programming comes from what I was doing on my spare time and from many hours spent on IRC channels.

I became interested in Python many years ago when I decided to write a little script for XChat IRC client, in order to have me automatically authenticated against the servers. The code was quite simple, but it sparked my curiosity and I decided to go a bit further and started using the language for automating all sorts of boring tasks.

Throughout my career in the IT Industry I've worked in the entire stack of software development, as frontend and backend engineer, systems and network administrator and also did a bit of mobile development. In the last company I worked for, I was both a senior backend engineer and the CTO.

Programming is one of my passions, but throughout the years I discovered that I'm as passionate about teaching and helping other people succeed as much as I am about programming. I've helped some friends make a career switch successfully and guided them through the process. This was one of the main reasons why I decided to quit my last job and fully dedicate myself to helping others do the same, either through e-books, tips and tricks, online courses or private coaching sessions.